# A Handbook of Types

*FOR THE AID OF TEACHERS WHO USE*
THE LOST TOOLS OF WRITING *LEVEL I*

© CiRCE Institute 2018

All rights reserved. No part of this publication may be reproduced, distributed, or transmitted in any form, by any means, including photocopying or other electronic, or mechanical methods, without the prior written consent of the publishers, except in the case of brief quotations embodied in critical reviews and other non-commerical uses permitted by copyright law.

For permission requests please write to the publisher: info@circeinstitute.com.

Cover design by Graeme Pitman. Printed in the USA.

# PERMISSIONS

Teachers who purchase or for whom schools purchase this *Handbook of Types* are granted permission to duplicate pages from the text for their personal use. Because this book accompanies *The Lost Tools of Writing* Level I, worksheets from the Handbook of Types can only be copied for those students who own the LTW I Student Workbook.

Permission is not granted to copy worksheets for students who do not own the LTW I Student Workbook.

Permission is granted for quotations and short excerpts to be used in published materials with the condition that the source of those quotations and excerpts is included in the published materials.

For longer excerpts, please contact us at www.circeinstitute.org.

# ACKNOWLEDGMENTS

Thousands of teachers and students have experienced *The Lost Tools of Writing*, and many have shared what a blessing it has been in their classrooms and homeschools. Many have so appreciated what it has has done for their students' writing and their own teaching, that they have asked for more types (examples) from different stories. Although we suspect some of you might just be a little tired of poor Edmund and his encounter with the White Witch!

This *Handbook of Types* is a response to that request, and as the Director of Curriculum—and therefore *The Lost Tools of Writing*—for the CiRCE Institute, I would like to acknowledge all of those who have had a hand in bringing this handbook to fruition.

Thank you to Buck Holler for his efforts in writing all of the types and examples. Thank you to Emily Dunnan for her fine editorial work. Thank you to David Kern for the beautiful and clean layout. Thank you to Graeme Pitman for anartful and beautiful cover.

We are especially thankful, though, to those who have given us the support, feedback, and suggestions that have made *The Lost Tools of Writing* and now the *Handbook of Types* the amazing resources they have become. We at the CiRCE Institute thank you for your generosity and support.

Matt Bianco
*Curriculum Director*
*CiRCE Institute*

# CONTENTS

**Preface - 6**

**Part I - Invention - II**
Essay One Invention: Question to ANI - 12
Essay Two Invention: Five Common Topics - 19
Essay Three Invention: Comparison I—Similarities - 23
Essay Four Invention: Comparison II—Differences - 27
Essay Five Invention: Definition - 31
Essay Six Invention: Circumstance - 35
Essay Seven Invention: Relation - 39
Essay Eight Invention: Authority - 43

**Part 2 - Arrangement - 47**
Essay One Arrangement: ANI to Outline - 49
Essay Two Arrangement: Sorting - 53
Essay Three Arrangement: Exordium - 63
Essay Four Arrangement: Amplification - 70
Essay Five Arrangement: Division - 77
Essay Six Arrangement: Refutation - 84
Essay Seven Arrangement: Narrative - 91
Essay Eight Arrangement: Review - 98

# CONTENTS

**Part 3 - Elocution - 99**

Essay One Elocution: Outline to Essay - 101

Essay Two Elocution: Parallelism I - 102

Essay Three Elocution: Verbs - 105

Essay Four Elocution: Parallelism II - 109

Essay Five Elocution: Antithesis - 112

Essay Six Elocution: Simile - 115

Essay Seven Elocution: Alliteration - 119

Essay Eight Elocution: Metaphor - 123

Essay Nine Elocution: Assonance - 127

**Part 4 - Essays - 131**

Essay One: Rudimentary Persuasive Essay - 133

Essay Two: Introductory Persuasive Essay - 137

Essay Three: Basic Persuasive Essay I - 141

Essay Four: Basic Persuasive Essay II - 145

Essay Five: Basic Persuasive Essay III - 149

Essay Six: Basic Persuasive Essay IV - 153

Essay Seven: Complete Persuasive Essay - 157

Essay Eight: Review Persuasive Essay - 162

Essay Nine: Review Persuasive Essay - 167

**Chapter 5 - Glossary - 173**

# PREFACE

I remember the day when I found myself sitting with a group of people whom I did not know in a room above a school gym discussing classical education. Suddenly the conversation shifted and we began discussing a writing curriculum I had never heard of. Soon I was told that I was to teach a lesson from this curriculum later in the week. I think it was on amplification. Afterwards, I was informed that my assignment was to return home and teach this to my students.

Such was my initiation to *The Lost Tools of Writing* (LTW). At the time, I had no idea why so much careful attention was dedicated to the understanding and teaching of this program or how it connected to classical education. Not long after, I began to see why. I began to see and experience how classical rhetoric improved my teaching because it drove me relentlessly to the heart of the lesson. The clearer my vision of the logos (idea) became, the clearer my teaching and my students' understanding became. Then I realized that classical rhetoric is the art of teaching and learning.

My experience teaching LTW has primarily taken place in the middle school classroom. Over the years, while teaching LTW, I was always looking for types. When traveling, I often came across other teachers of the program who were also looking for types. The idea of a handbook to accompany LTW by providing a catalogue of types that a teacher could pull into the lesson began to take shape. Thus, the goal for this handbook was to provide teachers of LTW with a resource to improve their own understanding of classical rhetoric and to complement their lessons with ready types.

I would like to add a few comments concerning the types used in the handbook, its overall design, and how the teacher might make the most use of it.

Notes on the types: The types are not perfect. I tried to capture some of the common things a teacher might see from students at different stages of the writing process. Sometimes students stumble onto parallelism with their proofs before you teach it. Sometimes a reason might fit into more than one category while sorting the ANI. Sometimes there are not enough reasons for a category after a student sorts the ANI. Often times the scheme or trope is not as great as expected.

The Invention types do not derive from the stories about which they are concerned. I did not look for definitions or comparisons in *The Wind in the Willows* or for circumstances in "Cinderella." They illustrate the process of inventing arguments from the stories by using the ANI and the five common topics.

Likewise, the types for Arrangement illustrate how to amplify the Rudimentary Persuasive Essay by adding a new part to the form of each new essay. In other words, the types for exordium are not exordia that I have pulled from Shakespeare's *Julius Caesar*. Rather, they are exordia that are composed in relation to the issue of whether Brutus should have stabbed Caesar.

The types for Elocution differ from Invention and Arrangement. Each section under Elocution consists of two parts. First, I pulled a total of 10 types from the three stories for each lesson in Elocution. Second, two additional constructed types for each story accompany the 10 model types.

General design. The handbook makes use of three classic texts: "Cinderella," *The Wind in the Willows*, and *Julius Caesar*. I intended these three texts to represent a beginning, middle, and advanced level of literature that may be used with students in grades 6 through 8. Each lesson within Invention, Arrangement, or Elocution contains types from all three books. A teacher preparing a lesson, for example, on definition will immediately find three types for definition: one from "Cinderella," one from *The Wind in the Willows*, and one from *Julius Caesar*.

Following the canons in the handbook is an additional chapter that contains essays one through nine. Again, each essay provides three types, one for each story. The teacher and students are able to observe how a simple rudimentary essay grows and develops as each new tool of rhetoric is appended to the Rudimentary Persuasive Essay. Finally, a glossary is provided for many of the common terms used in classical rhetoric and LTW.

Possible uses: Originally, I set out to compile a catalogue of types that the teacher could quickly refer to and pull from while preparing the lesson for the students. I found myself spending hours looking for types of exordia that I could use in my lessons. A handbook that contained several of these types would save much time and energy. Another use for the types in the handbook is strictly for the teacher. Even after several years of teaching LTW, I continually look to the types to reassure my understanding of the logos for the lesson I am preparing to teach. Types are embodiments of the logos, and good types lead one quickly to it. In his sixth letter to Lucilius, Seneca explains first that men give more credence to their eyes than to their ears, and secondly, *longum iter est per praecepta, breve et efficax per exempla* ("the way is long through precepts, but short and efficacious through examples").

My hope is that this handbook may amplify your understanding of LTW and complement the lessons you prepare to cultivate wisdom and virtue within your students.

*Buck Holler, April 2018*
*Head Mentor, CiRCE Institute Apprenticeship*
*LTW Development Team*

Part One
# Invention

# ESSAY ONE INVENTION: FROM QUESTION TO ANI

**Question:** Should . . .

**Issue:** Whether . . .

| A | N | I |
|---|---|---|
|   |   |   |

# Type A: From "Cinderella"

**Question:** Should Cinderella have gone to the celebration?

**Issue:** Whether Cinderella should have gone to the celebration

| A | N | I |
|---|---|---|
| She was beautiful | Stepmom told her to stay home | Cinderella was a daughter |
| King invited all beautiful girls | She did not have a dress | Cinderella was poor |
| Stepmother promised she could go | She did not pick the lentils | Her mother died |
| Birds gave her a dress | She did not know how to dance | Her father took a new wife who had two beautiful daughters |
| Birds helped her with the lentils | She was dirty | Stepsisters had ugly hearts |
| She does not have a husband | Needs to obey her parents | Stepmother hated Cinderella |
| Stepmother is cruel | She was poor | King wanted son to marry |
| Stepsisters are wicked | She lost her shoe | All beautiful girls invited to a celebration |
| Her father does not love her | Prince did not dance with other girls | C. picked lentils out of ashes |
| The prince chose to marry her | Mother told her to be good | A lentil is a bean |

**Sample Questions**

Who was Cinderella?
Who were the stepsisters?
What is a lentil?
What is a stepmother?
What is a celebration?
What did Cinderella and stepsisters have in common?
How do stepsisters differ from Cinderella?
How are C.'s mother and stepmother similar? Different?
What was happening at the grave during the celebration?
What was happening in kingdom?
What was happening at the celebration?
What did Cinderella do before the celebration?
What did Cinderella do after the celebration?
What did the stepmother do before the celebration?
What did the stepmother do after the celebration?
What did the stepmother tell Cinderella?
What did the prince tell the other maidens?
Who knows Cinderella the best?
Who saw Cinderella at the celebration?
Who knew Cinderella went to the celebration?

# Type B: From *The Wind in the Willows*

**Question:** Should Mole have left his home?

**Issue:** Whether Mole should have left his home

| A | N | I |
|---|---|---|
| He sensed something calling him | Mole fell into the river | Mole is a shy animal |
| He did not like spring cleaning | He is not done cleaning his house | Ratty lives on the riverbank |
| Mole met Ratty | Moles live under the ground | Toad has lots of money |
| Mole met new friends | He gets lost in the Wild Wood | Toad likes to do crazy things |
| Mole has a picnic with Ratty | The world is dangerous | Ratty is smart |
| To help Toad save his home | Mole is too impatient | Badger is old and wise |
| To meet Badger | He does not know what a river is | It was spring |
| To enjoy the spring | He has never been in a boat | No one goes to the Wide World |
| To experience the world above ground | Someone could take his home | Mole and Ratty have a picnic |
| He was alone | Toad gets into a lot of trouble | Mole tips Ratty's boat over |

**Sample Questions**

Who is Mole?
Who is Ratty?
What is a home?
What do Mole and Ratty have in common?
What do Mole and Toad have in common?
How does Mole differ from Ratty?
How are Mole's home and Toad Hall similar? Different?
How do Mole and Toad differ?
What was happening in Mole's home at the time?
What was happening outside of Mole's home?
What was happening on the riverbank?
What was happening at Toad Hall?
What happened before Mole left his home?
What happened after Mole left his home?
What did Mole do before leaving Ratty's home?
What did Mole and Ratty do after leaving the riverbank?
What does Ratty say about Mole's home?
What does Mole say about his home?
Why does Ratty say about the Wild Wood?
What does Ratty say about Toad Hall?

# Type C: From *Julius Caesar*

**Question:** Should Brutus have stabbed Caesar?

**Issue:** Whether Brutus should have stabbed Caesar

| A | N | I |
|---|---|---|
| To save Rome | Caesar trusted Brutus | Brutus was a senator |
| Brutus had support from other senators | Caesar was a hero | The citizens celebrated Caesar's return |
| Caesar threatened Rome's freedom | The people supported Caesar | Mark Antony competed in a race |
| The people wanted Caesar to be emperor | All the senators did not join the conspiracy | A soothsayer warned Caesar |
| To preserve liberty | No vote was taken among all the senators | Caesar did not like Cassius |
| Caesar was ambitious | Cassius was secretly plotting | Cassius helped Caesar in his weakness |
| Brutus loved Rome more | Caesar was Brutus' friend | Calpurnia had a dream |
| To distribute power | Caesar denied the crown | Calpurnia warned Caesar |
| Caesar brought his army into Rome | Cassius was seeking self-interests | Caesar trusted Brutus |
| The people offered Caesar the crown | Brutus was a respected leader of Rome | Caesar protected and defended Rome |

**Sample Questions**

Who was Brutus?
Who was Caesar?
What is an emperor?
What is Rome?
What did Brutus and Caesar have in common?
How does a senator differ from an emperor?
How are a friend and enemy similar? Different?
How do freedom and tyranny differ?
What was happening in the Senate at that time?
What was happening outside the Senate?
What was happening in Rome?
What had Caesar done in other parts of the empire?
Why was Caesar in Rome?
What caused Brutus to consider this act?
Why did some want Caesar dead?
What would his death cause?
What did Portia say to Brutus?
What did other senators advise Brutus?
Why did Brutus struggle with the decision?
What reason did any of the other senators have for their decision?

# ESSAY TWO INVENTION: THE FIVE COMMON TOPICS

**Topic of Comparison:**
How is X similar to Y?
How is X different from Y?

**Topic of Definition:**
Who or what is X?
What kind of thing or person is X?

**Topic of Circumstance:**
What was happening in the same place and time as your issue or situation?
What was happening at the same time as, but in different places from, your issue or situation?

**Topic of Relation:**
What led to the situation in which a decision needs to be made?
What followed the situation?

**Topic of Testimony:**
What do witnesses say about the character and/or his actions?

# Type A: From "Cinderella"

**Issue:** Whether Cinderella should have gone to the celebration

**Topic of Comparison:**
How is Cinderella similar to her stepsisters?
How is Cinderella different from her stepsisters?
How is the father similar to the king?
How is the father different from the king?

**Topic of Definition:**
What is a celebration?
Who is Cinderella?
What is a stepmother?
What is a prince? A king?

**Topic of Circumstance:**
What was happening during the celebration?
What was happening at Cinderella's house?
What was happening in the kingdom?
What was happening at Cinderella's mother's grave?

**Topic of Relation:**
What did Cinderella do before going to the celebration?
What did Cinderella do after leaving the celebration?
What did the stepmother do before the celebration?
What did the father do after the celebration?
What did the prince do after the celebration?

**Topic of Testimony:**
What does the father say about Cinderella?
What does the prince say about Cinderella?
What does the stepmother say about Cinderella?
What do the stepsisters say about Cinderella?
Who saw Cinderella at the celebration?

# Type B: From *The Wind in the Willows*

**Issue:** Whether Mole should have left his home

**Topic of Comparison:**
How are Mole and Ratty similar?
How are they different?
How are Mole and Toad similar?
How are they different?

**Topic of Definition:**
Who is Mole?
Who is Ratty?
What is a home?
Who is Toad?
Who is Badger?

**Topic of Circumstance:**
What is happening at the time Mole leaves his home?
What is happening in Mole's burrow?
What is happening above ground near Mole's burrow?
What is happening on the riverbank?
What is happening at Toad hall?
What is happening in the Wild Wood?
What is happening in the Wide World?

**Topic of Relation:**
What happened just before Mole left his home?
What happened just after he left?
What did Mole do before leaving his home?
What did Mole do before leaving Ratty's home?
What did Mole and Ratty do after leaving the riverbank?

**Topic of Testimony:**
What does Ratty say about Mole's home?
What does Ratty say about the riverbank?
What does Ratty say about the Wild Wood?
What does Badger say about the Wild Wood?
What does Ratty say about the Wide World?

# Type B: From *Julius Caesar*

**Issue:** Whether Brutus should have stabbed Julius Caesar

**Topic of Comparison:**
What do Brutus and Caesar have in common?
How do Brutus and Caesar differ?
How does a senator differ from an emperor?
How are a friend and enemy similar? How are they different?
How do freedom and tyranny differ?

**Topic of Definition:**
Who is Brutus?
Who is Julius Caesar?
What kind of person is Caesar?
What is an emperor?
What are the characteristics of a Roman?
What is murder?

**Topic of Circumstance:**
What was happening in the Senate at that time?
What was happening outside the Senate at the same time?
What was happening in Gaul at the same time?

**Topic of Relation:**
What happened before the time with which the issue of stabbing Caesar is concerned?
What happened immediately afterward?
Why was Caesar in Rome?
What led Cassius to come to Brutus with his plan?
What followed the suggestion of stabbing Caesar?
What followed the senators' plot?

**Topic of Testimony:**
What do Brutus' friends say about him?
What do Caesar's friends say about him?
What do others say about Caesar?
Who saw Brutus stab Caesar?
What does Cassius say about Brutus stabbing Caesar?
What does Antony say about Brutus stabbing Caesar?

# *ESSAY THREE INVENTION: COMPARISON I—SIMILARITIES*

List the two terms you will compare:

**Term A:**

**Term B:**

| What do both have? | What are both? | What do both do? |
|---|---|---|
|  |  |  |

# Type A: From "Cinderella"

List the two terms you will compare:

**Term A:** Cinderella

**Term B:** Stepsisters

| What do both have? | What are both? | What do both do? |
|---|---|---|
| one parent<br>one stepparent<br>desire<br>feet<br>dresses | beautiful<br>daughters<br>young girls<br>unmarried<br>stepsisters | go to the celebration<br>seek to marry the prince<br>put on the shoe<br>ask the father for gifts<br>live in the same house |

Type B: From *The Wind in the Willows*

List the two terms you will compare:

**Term A:** Mole

**Term B:** Toad

| What do both have? | What are both? | What do both do? |
|---|---|---|
| house<br>friends<br>desires<br>need for help<br>enemies | animals<br>impatient<br>kind<br>fun<br>adventurous<br>friends | live adventurously<br>travel<br>leave home<br>get in trouble<br>find help |

## Type C: From *Julius Caesar*

List the two terms you will compare:

**Term A:** Brutus

**Term B:** Caesar

| What do both have? | What are both? | What do both do? |
|---|---|---|
| wives<br>friends<br>money<br>power<br>authority<br>passions | men<br>Romans<br>leaders<br>husbands<br>friends | talk<br>seek advice<br>listen<br>go to the Senate<br>lead men |

# ESSAY FOUR INVENTION: COMPARISON II—DIFFERENCES

List the two terms you will compare:

**Term A:**  **Term B:**

| | | |
|---|---|---|
| **BOTH A & B DO (LIST VERBS)** | A does more/less_____ than B (describe the difference) | A does _____ better/worse than B (describe the difference). |
| | | |
| **BOTH A & B HAVE (LIST NOUNS BOTH HAVE)** | A has more/less_____ than B (describe the difference). | A has better/worse _____ than B (describe the difference). |
| | | |
| **BOTH A & B ARE (LIST ADJECTIVES BOTH SHARE)** | A is more_____ than B (describe the difference). | |
| | | |
| **BOTH A & B ARE (LIST GROUPS BOTH BELONG TO)** | | A is a better/worse _____ than B (describe the difference). |
| | | |

# Type A: From "Cinderella"

List the two terms you will compare:

**Term A: Cinderella**     **Term B: Stepsisters**

| **BOTH A & B DO (LIST VERBS)** | A does more/less _____ than B (describe the difference) | A does _____ better/worse than B (describe the difference). |
|---|---|---|
| go to the celebration<br>seek to marry the prince<br>put on the shoe<br>ask the father for gifts<br>live in the same house | *Stepsisters ask the father for more expensive gifts than Cinderella*<br><br>*Stepsisters seek marriage more than Cinderella, mutilating their feet to fit the shoe* | *Cinderella puts on the shoe better because it fits her foot*<br><br>*Cinderella asks for a better gift than the stepsisters, which becomes a tree giving better advice, dresses, and help* |
| **BOTH A & B HAVE (LIST NOUNS BOTH HAVE)** | A has more/less _____ than B (describe the difference). | A has better/worse _____ than B (describe the difference). |
| one parent<br>one stepparent<br>desire<br>feet<br>dresses | *Stepsisters have less of a foot than Cinderella because they cut parts off*<br><br>*Cinderella's dress is more radiant than the others* | *Cinderella has a better dress than stepsisters*<br><br>*Cinderella has a better desire for marriage than the stepsisters who want wealth* |
| **BOTH A & B ARE (LIST ADJECTIVES BOTH SHARE)** | A is more _____ than B (describe the difference). | |
| beautiful<br>young | *Cinderella is more beautiful than the stepsisters because their beauty is only on the outside while their hearts are ugly and black* | |
| **BOTH A & B ARE (LIST GROUPS BOTH BELONG TO)** | | A is a better/worse _____ than B (describe the difference). |
| daughters<br>unmarried<br>stepsisters | | *Cinderella is a better stepsister because she tries to help and please others*<br><br>*Cinderella is a better daughter because she tries to be good* |

# Type B: From *The Wind in the Willows*

List the two terms you will compare:

**Term A: Mole**     **Term B: Toad**

| | | |
|---|---|---|
| **BOTH A & B DO (LIST VERBS)** | A does more/less_____ than B (describe the difference) | A does _____ better/worse than B (describe the difference). |
| live adventurously<br>travel<br>leave home<br>get in trouble<br>find help | Toad lives more adventurously than Mole because he does not try to be safe<br><br>Toad gets in more trouble than Mole by the police and is thrown in jail | Toad gets in worse trouble than Mole because he goes to jail<br><br>Mole lives better than Toad because he stays in control of his wants and desires |
| **BOTH A & B HAVE (LIST NOUNS BOTH HAVE)** | A has more/less_____ than B (describe the difference). | A has better/worse _____ than B (describe the difference). |
| house<br>friends<br>desires<br>need for help<br>enemies | Toad's house is bigger than Moles and has more stuff<br><br>Toad needs more help than Mole because he gets in more trouble | Toad has a better house than Mole because Mole's house is small, dirty, and underground<br><br>Toad has worse desires than Mole because he steals a car |
| **BOTH A & B ARE (LIST ADJECTIVES BOTH SHARE)** | A is more_____ than B (describe the difference). | |
| impatient<br>kind<br>fun<br>adventurous | Toad is more impatient than Mole because he changes his mind more<br><br>Toad is more adventurous than Mole because he does dangerous things | |
| **BOTH A & B ARE (LIST GROUPS BOTH BELONG TO)** | | A is a better/worse _____ than B (describe the difference). |
| animals<br>friends | | Mole is a better friend than Toad because he helps Toad save his house |

# Type C: From *Julius Caesar*

List the two terms you will compare:

**Term A: Brutus**    **Term B: Caesar**

| **BOTH A & B DO (LIST VERBS)** | A does more/less_____ than B (describe the difference) | A does _____ better/worse than B (describe the difference). |
|---|---|---|
| talk<br>seek advice<br>listen<br>go to the Senate<br>lead men | *Brutus listens to others more than Caesar; leads fewer men than Caesar; seeks worse advice*<br><br>*Caesar listens to others less than Brutus; leads more men than Brutus; receives better advice* | *Brutus seeks worse advice than Caesar*<br><br>*Caesar receives better advice than Brutus* |
| **BOTH A & B HAVE (LIST NOUNS BOTH HAVE)** | A has more/less_____ than B (describe the difference). | A has better/worse _____ than B (describe the difference). |
| wives<br>friends<br>money<br>power<br>authority<br>passions | *Brutus has less authority than Caesar; more friends in the Senate than Caesar*<br><br>*Caesar has more authority than Brutus* | *Brutus has worse friends than Caesar who are dishonest*<br><br>*Caesar has better friends than Brutus who are loyal, such as Antony* |
| **BOTH A & B ARE (LIST ADJECTIVES BOTH SHARE)** | A is more_____ than B (describe the difference). | |
| Romans | *Brutus is more honorable than Caesar*<br><br>*Caesar is a more ambitious leader than Brutus* | *Brutus listens to dishonorable plans to kill Caesar; bad advice*<br><br>*Caesar ignores good advice from his wife* |
| **BOTH A & B ARE (LIST GROUPS BOTH BELONG TO)** | | A is a better/worse _____ than B (describe the difference). |
| men<br>leaders<br>husbands<br>friends | | *Brutus is a worse friend than Caesar; worse leader*<br><br>*Caesar is a better friend; better leader* |

# ESSAY FIVE INVENTION: DEFINITION

Identify a **term** from your issue.

List three or four **groups** this term belongs to.

Select a **group** from the list above which will be helpful for you as you define the term.

List other **members** (three or four) of the group you selected.

Identify a **common** characteristic of all members of this group (What quality do all the members share?).

What characteristic makes the term **different** from these other group members?

Write your **definition**. Include the term, its group, and its difference. In other words, state that the term is a member of its group and how it is different from all the other members.

## Type A: From "Cinderella"

**Term:** celebration

**Groups:** special event, party, festival, assembly

**Choose a group:** special event

**Other members of this group:** wedding, birthday party, funeral, graduation

**Common characteristic:** rare occasions, happen yearly or once, guests, invitations, food, drinks, emotions

**Unique characteristic:** declared by the king to find his son a wife

**Definition:** The celebration in "Cinderella" was a special event declared by the king to find his son a wife.

Type B: From *Wind in the Willows*

**Term:** home

**Groups:** building, shelter, protection, place

**Choose a group:** shelter

**Other members of this group:** cave, tent, barn, shed, ditch, container, hole

**Common characteristic:** protect against weather, intruders, attacks from enemies

**Unique characteristic:** place of belonging, personal, gives comfort and peace

**Definition:** A home is a shelter that gives comfort and peace to its inhabitant.

# Type C: From *Julius Caesar*

**Term:** Caesar

**Groups:** man, leader, friend, husband, Roman

**Choose a group:** leader

**Other members of this group:** Brutus, Cassius, Marc Anthony

**Common characteristic:** Romans, possess strong passions, concerned about power, freedom, and tyranny

**Unique characteristic:** possess authority that generates love and fear

**Definition:** Caesar was a Roman military leader whose authority generated love and fear.

# ***ESSAY SIX INVENTION: CIRCUMSTANCE***

Issue:

Situation:

List actions and events that occur at the same time but in different locations surrounding your issue.

Location 1:

Location 2:

Location 3:

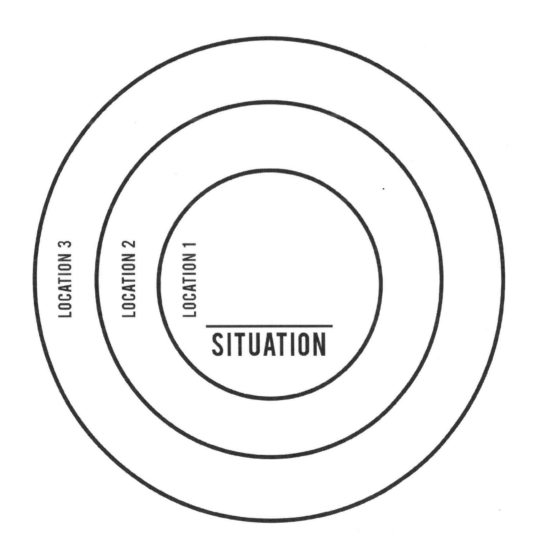

## Type A: From "Cinderella"

**Issue:** Whether Cinderella should have gone to the celebration

**Situation:** King declared a celebration to find his son a wife; all beautiful girls in the kingdom were invited; Cinderella was told to stay home by her stepmother; Cinderella was sad, dirty, and without a dress

List actions and events that occur at the same time but in different **locations** surrounding your issue.

**Location 1:** The stepmother and two stepsisters hurry away to the king's palace leaving Cinderella at home

**Location 2:** Many girls who live in the kingdom are at the celebration to meet the prince; the prince attends the celebration to find a bride

**Location 3:** Cinderella goes to her mother's grave; she cries under the hazel tree at her mother's grave; a bird tosses down a beautiful dress

# Type B: From *The Wind in the Willows*

**Issue:** Whether Mole should have left his home

**Situation:** Mole is cleaning his house; it is springtime and he is feeling an urge to leave his home; he does not like cleaning

List actions and events that occur at the same time but in different **locations** surrounding your issue.

**Location 1:** Mole is underground in his home cleaning

**Location 2:** Outside spring has arrived and all the animals are enjoying the day

**Location 3:** Ratty is relaxing on the river

# Type C: From *Julius Caesar*

**Issue:** Whether Brutus should have stabbed Caesar

**Situation:** Ides of March, 43 B.C.; city of Rome; Caesar has returned from northern conquests; people want to make Caesar Emperor; Caesar goes before the Senate to receive a crown

List actions and events that occur at the same time but in different **locations** surrounding your issue.

**Location 1:** Inside the Senate, several senators distract Caesar with questions concerning Cimber's banished brother; Caesar remarks how constant he is in his decisions

**Location 2:** Outside the Senate, the people are rejoicing in Caesar's triumphs upon his return; a soothsayer told Caesar that the Ides of March are not yet gone; Artemidorus attempted to warn Caesar by pressing him to read a letter

**Location 3:** Outside of Rome, the empire is currently at rest and under Roman governance due to Caesar's successful conquests

# ESSAY SEVEN INVENTION: RELATION

Issue:

Describe the situation in which the actor finds himself.

List several actions or events that preceded this situation.

Select and circle or underline several causes or probable causes of the situation.

List several actions or events that followed or will likely follow the affirmative decision.

List several actions or events that followed or will likely follow the negative decision.

Select and circle or underline several effects or probable effects of each decision.

# Type A: From "Cinderella"

**Issue:** Whether Cinderella should have gone to the celebration

**Describe the situation in which the actor finds himself.**
The king declared a celebration to find his son a wife; all beautiful girls in the kingdom were invited; Cinderella was told to stay home by her stepmother; Cinderella was sad, dirty, and without a dress

**List several actions or events that preceded this situation.**
Cinderella's mother died
Her father remarried
<u>The new wife has two beautiful daughters who mistreat Cinderella</u>
Cinderella must pick lentils out of the ashes
Birds help Cinderella pick lentils out of the ashes
<u>Stepsisters took away Cinderella's fine clothes and gave her rags and wooden shoes</u>
Stepsisters laughed at Cinderella
<u>Cinderella slept in the ashes</u>
<u>Cinderella asked stepmother if she could go to the celebration</u>

**Select and circle or underline several causes or probable causes of the situation.**

**List several actions or events that followed or will likely follow the affirmative decision.**
<u>The prince will marry Cinderella</u>
<u>She will have a new home</u>
She will have better clothes
Cinderella will not have to pick lentils anymore
<u>Stepmother and stepsisters will be angry with her</u>

**List several actions or events that followed or will likely follow the negative decision.**
Prince will marry someone else
<u>Cinderella will continue living in poverty</u>
She will not receive new clothes
She will still sleep in the lentils
<u>Her stepsisters will continue making fun of her</u>

**Select and circle or underline several effects or probable effects of each decision.**

# Type B: From *The Wind in the Willows*

**Issue:** Whether Mole should have left his home

**Describe the situation in which the actor finds himself.**
Mole is cleaning his house; it is springtime and he is feeling an urge to leave his home; he does not like cleaning

**List several actions or events that preceded this situation.**
It was winter
<u>Mole's house is dirty</u>
Mole begins cleaning his house
<u>Mole had an urge to leave home</u>

**Select and circle or underline several causes or probable causes of the situation.**

**List several actions or events that followed or will likely follow the affirmative decision.**
Meet new friends
<u>Have adventures</u>
Learn to go up and down the river
<u>Enjoy the sunshine</u>
Play in the fields
Have fun
<u>See and explore new places</u>

**List several actions or events that followed or will likely follow the negative decision.**
Won't get lost
<u>Won't get into trouble</u>
Won't get hurt
<u>House might get cleaned</u>
Won't broaden his horizons

**Select and circle or underline several effects or probable effects of each decision.**

# Type C: From *Julius Caesar*

**Issue:** Whether Brutus should have stabbed Caesar

**Describe the situation in which the actor finds himself.**
Brutus has been approached by senators to join their plot to assassinate Caesar; Brutus is a friend of Caesar, but he does not want to lose the Republic; Brutus stabbed Caesar

**List several actions or events that preceded this situation.**
Caesar returned to Rome
People celebrated in the streets
<u>The senators fear Caesar, tyranny, and the loss of freedom</u>
Caesar denied the crown during the games
Soothsayer told Caesar to beware the Ides of March
<u>Cassius secretly met with Brutus to gain his support</u>

**Select and circle or underline several causes or probable causes of the situation.**

**List several actions or events that followed or will likely follow the affirmative decision.**
The people of Rome will revolt
<u>Mourning over Caesar's death</u>
Senators exiled
<u>War or conflict with Caesar's supporters</u>
Death

**List several actions or events that followed or will likely follow the negative decision.**
Gain enemies among the senators conspiring to assassinate Caesar
Caesar accepts a crown
<u>Tyranny or a virtuous emperor who is both respected and loved</u>
Friendship with and loyalty to Caesar
<u>Stability</u>
Peace in the streets of Rome

**Select and circle or underline several effects or probable effects of each decision.**

# ***ESSAY EIGHT INVENTION: TESTIMONY***

Describe the situation of the issue:

**Witness #1: Eyewitness**

Name an eyewitness.

What has this witness seen the actor do or experience in this situation?

How reliable do you consider this witness? Mostly reliable/mostly unreliable

**Witness #2: Character Witness**

Name a person who knows something about the character of an actor(s) in this situation.

About whose character can he testify?

What did the witness observe and in what circumstances did he observe it?

What does that suggest about the character of the actor?

How do these observations relate to the situation?

How reliable do you consider this witness? Mostly reliable/mostly unreliable

# Type A: From "Cinderella"

**Describe the situation of the issue:**
The king declared a celebration to find his son a wife; all beautiful girls in the kingdom are invited; Cinderella was told to stay home by her stepmother; Cinderella was sad, dirty, and without a dress

## Witness #1: Eyewitness

**Name an eyewitness:** Stepsisters

**What has this witness seen the actor do or experience in this situation?**
Cinderella dressed in rags cleaning lentils
Their mother promising Cinderella that she could go if she finished her task, and then break that promise
Their mother mistreat and lie to Cinderella

**How reliable do you consider this witness? Mostly reliable/mostly unreliable?**
Mostly unreliable

## Witness #2: Character Witness

**Name a person who knows something about the character of an actor(s) in this situation:**
Cinderella

**About whose character can she testify?** Stepmother

**What did the witness observe and in what circumstances did she observe it?**
Her stepmother broke a promise; the stepmother told Cinderella she could go to the celebration if she cleaned all the lentils within an hour. When the task was complete, the stepmother changed her mind and told Cinderella she could not go to the celebration.

**What does that suggest about the character of the actor?**
She is dishonest

**How do these observations relate to the situation?**
Cinderella needs to decide if she should go to the celebration. The king has invited her, but her stepmother has told her to stay home.

**How reliable do you consider this witness? Mostly reliable/mostly unreliable?**
Mostly reliable

# Type B: From *The Wind in the Willows*

**Describe the situation of the issue:**
Mole is cleaning his house; it is springtime and he is feeling an urge to leave his home; he does not like cleaning

### Witness #1: Eyewitness

**Name an eyewitness:** Ratty

**What has this witness seen the actor do or experience in this situation?**
Not listen to advice
Act impatiently without thinking
Try to learn
Ask for help

**How reliable do you consider this witness? Mostly reliable/mostly unreliable?**
Mostly reliable

### Witness #2: Character Witness

**Name a person who knows something about the character of an actor(s) in this situation:**
Ratty

**About whose character can he testify?** Mole

**What did the witness observe and in what circumstances did he observe it?**
Ratty witnessed Mole taking control of the boat after he told Mole that he was not ready; Mole ended up tipping the boat over in the river and Ratty had to help him out of the river

**What does that suggest about the character of the actor?**
Mole does not think before he acts

**How do these observations relate to the situation?**
Mole needs to carefully think about leaving home; without help, he might get into a lot of trouble

**How reliable do you consider this witness? Mostly reliable/mostly unreliable?**
Mostly reliable

# Type C: From *Julius Caesar*

**Describe the situation of the issue:**
Brutus and a group of senators stabbed Caesar in the Senate to save the Republic from tyranny

### Witness #1: Eyewitness

**Name an eyewitness:** Publica

**What has this witness seen the actor do or experience in this situation?**
The senators distract Caesar with pleas
Senators stab Caesar
Brutus joins in the stabbing
Struck with fear, confusion, and confounded by the mutiny

**How reliable do you consider this witness? Mostly reliable/mostly unreliable?**
Mostly reliable

### Witness #2: Character Witness

**Name a person who knows something about the character of an actor(s) in this situation:**
Cassius

**About whose character can he testify?** Brutus

**What did the witness observe and in what circumstances did he observe it?**
He has seen how the people respect and honor Brutus

**What does that suggest about the character of the actor?**
Brutus is a man of honor

**How do these observations relate to the situation?**
Cassius believes that Brutus will do what is best for the Republic and support the conspirators' cause

**How reliable do you consider this witness? Mostly reliable/mostly unreliable?**
Mostly reliable

# Part Two
# Arrangement

# ESSAY ONE ARRANGEMENT: ANI TO OUTLINE

I. Introduction
   A. Thesis
   B. Enumeration
   C. Exposition
      1.
      2.
      3.

II. Proof
   A.
   B.
   C.

III. Conclusion
   A. Thesis
   B. Summary of Proof
      1.
      2.
      3.

Type A: From "Cinderella"

I. Introduction

    A. Thesis: **Cinderella should have gone to the celebration**

    B. Enumeration: **for three reasons**

    C. Exposition

        1. **All beautiful girls, king invited**
        2. **Stepmother promised could go**
        3. **No husband**

II. Proof

    A. **All beautiful girls, king invited**

    B. **Stepmother promised could go**

    C. **No husband**

III. Conclusion

    A. Thesis: **Cinderella should have gone to the celebration**

    B. Summary of Proof

        1. **All beautiful girls, king invited**
        2. **Stepmother promised could go**
        3. **No husband**

# Type B: From *The Wind in the Willows*

I. Introduction

    A. Thesis: **Mole should have left his home**

    B. Enumeration: **for three reasons**

    C. Exposition

        1. **Alone**
        2. **Not like spring cleaning**
        3. **Met new friends**

II. Proof

    A. **Alone**

    B. **Not like spring cleaning**

    C. **Met new friends**

III. Conclusion

    A. Thesis: **Mole should have left his home**

    B. Summary of Proof

        1. **Alone**
        2. **Not like spring cleaning**
        3. **Met new friends**

# Type C: From *Julius Caesar*

I. Introduction

    A. Thesis: **Brutus should not have stabbed Caesar**

    B. Enumeration: **for three reasons**

    C. Exposition

        1. **Trusted Brutus**
        2. **People supported**
        3. **Brutus respected leader**

II. Proof

    A. **Trusted Brutus**

    B. **People supported**

    C. **Brutus respected leader**

III. Conclusion

    A. Thesis: **Brutus should not have stabbed Caesar**

    B. Summary of Proof

        1. **Trusted Brutus**
        2. **People supported**
        3. **Brutus respected leader**

# ***ESSAY TWO ARRANGEMENT: SORTING***

I. Introduction

    A. Thesis
    B. Enumeration
    C. Exposition
        1.
        2.
        3.

II. Proof

    A. Proof 1
        **1. support for proof 1**
        **2. support for proof 1**
        **3. support for proof 1**

    B. Proof 2
        **1. support for proof 2**
        **2. support for proof 2**
        **3. support for proof 2**

    C. Proof 3
        **1. support for proof 3**
        **2. support for proof 3**
        **3. support for proof 3**

III. Conclusion

    A. Thesis
    B. Summary of Proof
        1.
        2.
        3.

# Type A: From "Cinderella"

**Step One: Identify Groups**

| A Column | | N Column | |
|---|---|---|---|
| @ | She was beautiful | * | Stepmom told her to stay home |
| @& | King invited all beautiful girls | % | She did not have a dress |
| # | Stepmother promised she could go | % | She did not pick the lentils |
| # | Birds gave her a dress | % | She did not know how to dance |
| # | Birds helped her with the lentils | # | She was dirty |
| & | She does not have a husband | * | Needs to obey her parents |
| % | Stepmother is cruel | # | She was poor |
| % | Stepsisters are wicked | % | She lost her shoe |
| % | Her father does not love her | $ | Prince did not dance with other girls |
| & | The prince chose to marry her | * | Mother told her to be good |

**Step Two: Regroup**

| A Column | | N Column | |
|---|---|---|---|
| @ | She was beautiful | * | Stepmom told her to stay home |
| @& | King invited all beautiful girls | * | Needs to obey her parents |
| | | * | Mother told her to be good |
| @& | King invited all beautiful girls | | |
| & | She does not have a husband | % | She did not have a dress |
| & | The prince chose to marry her | % | She did not pick the lentils |
| | | % | She did not know how to dance |
| # | Stepmother promised she could go | | |
| # | Birds gave her a dress | # | She was dirty |
| # | Birds helped her with the lentils | # | She was poor |
| % | Stepmother is cruel | $ | Prince did not dance with other girls |
| % | Stepsisters are wicked | | |
| % | Her father does not love her | | |

54

**Step Three: Label Each Group**

*A Column*

Beauty
@     She was beautiful
@&    King invited all beautiful girls

Marriage
@&    King invited all beautiful girls
&     She does not have a husband
&     The prince chose to marry her

Permission
#     Stepmother promised she could go
#     Birds gave her a dress
#     Birds helped her with the lentils

Family
%     Stepmother is cruel
%     Stepsisters are wicked
%     Her father does not love her

*N Column*

Follow Instructions
*     Stepmom told her to stay home
*     Needs to obey her parents
*     Mother told her to be good

Not Ready
%     She did not have a dress
%     She did not pick the lentils
%     She did not know how to dance

Condition
#     She was dirty
#     She was poor

Dance
$     Prince did not dance with other girls

**Step Four: Select Groups (Proofs)**

A or N?: A

Thesis: Cinderella should have gone to the celebration

Proof A: Marriage
    1. King invited all beautiful girls
    2. She does not have a husband
    3. The prince chose to marry her

Proof B: Permission
    1. Stepmother promised she could go
    2. Birds gave her a dress
    3. Birds helped her with the lentils

Proof C: Family
    1. Stepmother is cruel
    2. Stepsisters are wicked
    3. Her father does not love her

# Outline

I. Introduction

    A. Thesis: Cinderella should have gone to the celebration

    B. Enumeration: for three reasons

    C. Exposition

        1. Marriage
        2. Permission
        3. Family

II. Proof

    A. Marriage
        **1. All beautiful girls, king invited**
        **2. No husband**
        **3. Prince chose**

    B. Permission
        **1. Stepmother promised**
        **2. Birds gave dress**
        **3. Birds helped**

    C. Family
        **1. Stepmother cruel**
        **2. Stepsisters wicked**
        **3. Not loved by father**

III. Conclusion

    A. Thesis: Cinderella should have gone to the celebration
    B. Summary of Proof

        1. Marriage
        2. Permission
        3. Family

# Type B: From *The Wind in the Willows*

## Step One: Identify Groups

| | A Column | | N Column |
|---|---|---|---|
| @ | He sensed something calling him | * | Mole fell into the river |
| #@ | He did not like spring cleaning | @ | He is not done cleaning his house |
| % | Mole met Ratty | # | Moles live under the ground |
| % | Mole met new friends | * | He gets lost in the Wild Wood |
| & | Mole has a picnic with Ratty | * | The world is dangerous |
| & | To help Toad save his home | @ | Mole is too impatient |
| % | To meet Badger | # | He does not know what a river is |
| @ | To enjoy the spring | # | He has never been in a boat |
| @ | To experience the world above ground | * | Someone could take his home |
| % | He was alone | % | Toad gets into a lot of trouble |
| & | To go on a road trip with Ratty and Toad | @# | His home is safe |
| & | To have lunch at Toad Hall | @ | He is easily distracted |

## Step Two: Regroup

| | A Column | | N Column |
|---|---|---|---|
| @ | He sensed something calling him | * | Mole fell into the river |
| #@ | He did not like spring cleaning | * | He gets lost in the Wild Wood |
| @ | To enjoy the spring | * | The world is dangerous |
| @ | To experience the world above ground | * | Someone could take his home |
| | | | |
| % | Mole met Ratty | @ | He is not done cleaning his house |
| % | Mole met new friends | @ | Mole is too impatient |
| % | To meet Badger | @# | His home is safe |
| % | He was alone | @ | He is easily distracted |
| | | | |
| #@ | He did not like spring cleaning | # | Moles live under the ground |
| | | # | He does not know what a river is |
| | | # | He has never been in a boat |
| | | @# | His home is safe |
| & | Mole has a picnic with Ratty | | |
| & | To help Toad save his home | % | Toad gets into a lot of trouble |
| & | To go on a road trip with Ratty and Toad | | |
| & | To have lunch at Toad Hall | | |

**Step Three: Label Each Group**

               *A Column*                              *N Column*

<u>Spring</u>
- @     He sensed something calling him
- #@   He did not like spring cleaning
- @     To enjoy the spring
- @     To experience the world above ground

<u>Friends</u>
- %     Mole met Ratty
- %     Mole met new friends
- %     To meet Badger
- %     He was alone

<u>Cleaning</u>
- #@   He did not like spring cleaning

<u>New Adventures</u>
- &     Mole has a picnic with Ratty
- &     To help Toad save his home
- &     To go on a road trip with Ratty and Toad
- &     To have lunch at Toad Hall

<u>Dangers</u>
- \*     Mole fell into the river
- \*     He gets lost in the Wild Wood
- \*     The world is dangerous
- \*     Someone could take his home

<u>Impatient</u>
- @     He is not done cleaning his house
- @     Mole is too impatient
- @#   His home is safe
- @     He is easily distracted

<u>Unknown World</u>
- #     Moles live under the ground
- #     He does not know what a river is
- #     He has never been in a boat
- @#   His home is safe

<u>Trouble</u>
- %     Toad gets into a lot of trouble

**Step Four: Select Groups (Proofs)**

A or N? A

Thesis: Mole should have left his house.

Proof A: Spring
1. He sensed something calling him
2. To enjoy the spring
3. To experience the world above ground

Proof B: Friends
1. He was alone
2. Mole met Ratty
3. To meet Badger

Proof C: New Adventures
1. To have lunch at Toad Hall
2. To go on a road trip with Ratty and Toad
3. To help Toad save his home

# Outline

I. Introduction

    A. Thesis: Mole should have left his home

    B. Enumeration: for three reasons

    C. Exposition
        1. Spring
        2. Friends
        3. New adventures

II. Proof

    A: Spring
        **1. Sensed something calling**
        **2. Enjoy spring**
        **3. Experience the world above**

    B. Friends
        **1. Alone**
        **2. Met Ratty**
        **3. To meet Badger**

    C. New Adventures
        **1. To lunch at Toad Hall**
        **2. To go on a road trip with Ratty and Toad**
        **3. To help Toad save his home**

III. Conclusion

    A. Thesis: Mole should have left his home

    B. Summary of Proof
        1. Spring
        2. Friends
        3. New Adventures

# Type C: From *Julius Caesar*

## Step One: Identify Groups

| A Column | | N Column | |
|---|---|---|---|
| @ | To save Rome | ^ | Caesar trusted Brutus |
| $ | Brutus had support from other senators | * | Caesar was a hero |
| @ # | Caesar threatened Rome's freedom | * | The people supported Caesar |
| % | People wanted Caesar to be emperor | $ | All the senators did not join conspiracy |
| @ | To preserve liberty | $ | No vote was taken among all senators |
| # | Caesar was ambitious | ! | Cassius was secretly plotting |
| @ | Brutus loved Rome more | ^ | Caesar was Brutus' friend |
| % | To distribute power | * | Caesar denied the crown |
| # | Caesar brought his army into Rome | ! | Cassius was seeking self-interests |
| % | The people offered Caesar the crown | ^ | Brutus was a respected leader of Rome |
| | | $ | Many senators were not aware of the plot |

## Step Two: Regroup

| A Column | | N Column | |
|---|---|---|---|
| @ | To save Rome | ^ | Caesar trusted Brutus |
| @ # | Caesar threatened Rome's freedom | ^ | Caesar was Brutus' friend |
| @ | To preserve liberty | ^ | Brutus was a respected leader of Rome |
| @ | Brutus loved Rome more | | |
| | | * | Caesar was a hero |
| $ | Brutus had support from other senators | * | The people supported Caesar |
| | | * | Caesar denied the crown |
| @ # | Caesar threatened Rome's freedom | | |
| # | Caesar was ambitious | $ | All the senators did not join conspiracy |
| # | Caesar brought his army into Rome | $ | No vote was taken among all the senators |
| | | $ | Many senators were not aware of the plot |
| % | The people wanted Caesar to be emperor | | |
| % | To distribute power | ! | Cassius was secretly plotting |
| % | The people offered Caesar the crown | ! | Cassius was seeking self-interests |

**Step Three: Label Each Group**

*A Column*

For Rome
@       To save Rome
@ #    Caesar threatened Rome's freedom
@       To preserve liberty
@       Brutus loved Rome more

Support
$       Brutus had support from other senators

Caesar's Lust for Power
@ #    Caesar threatened Rome's freedom
#       Caesar was ambitious
#       Caesar brought his army into Rome

Weaken Caesar's Power
%      The people wanted Caesar to be emperor
%      To distribute power
%      The people offered Caesar the crown

*N Column*

Brutus is Trustworthy
^       Caesar trusted Brutus
^       Caesar was Brutus' friend
^       Brutus was a respected leader of Rome

Caesar Earned the People's Favor
*       Caesar was a hero
*       The people supported Caesar
*       Caesar denied the crown

The Senate
$       All the senators did not join conspiracy
$       No vote was taken among all the senators
$       Many senators were not aware of the plot

The Plot of Cassius
!       Cassius was secretly plotting
!       Cassius was seeking self-interests

**Step Four: Select Groups (Proofs)**

A or N? N

Thesis: Brutus should not have stabbed Caesar.

Proof A: Brutus is Trustworthy
     1. Caesar trusted Brutus
     2. Caesar was Brutus' friend
     3. Brutus was a respected leader of Rome

Proof B: Caesar Earned the People's Favor
     1. Caesar was a hero
     2. The people supported Caesar
     3. Caesar denied the crown

Proof C: The Senate
     1. All the senators did not join the conspiracy
     2. No vote was taken among all the senators
     3. Many senators were not aware of the plot

# Outline

I. Introduction

    A. Thesis: Brutus should not have stabbed Caesar

    B. Enumeration: for three reasons

    C. Exposition
        1. Brutus
        2. Caesar
        3. Senate

II. Proof

    A. Brutus
        **1. Caesar trusted**
        **2. Caesar's friend**
        **3. Respected leader of Rome**

    B. Caesar
        **1. A hero**
        **2. The people supported**
        **3. Denied the crown**

    C. Senate
        **1. All did not join the conspiracy**
        **2. No vote**
        **3. Many not aware of plot**

III. Conclusion

    A. Thesis: Brutus should not have stabbed Caesar

    B. Summary of Proof
        1. Brutus
        2. Caesar
        3. Senate

# ***ESSAY THREE ARRANGEMENT: EXORDIUM***

I.  Introduction

    **A. Exordium**
    B.  Thesis
    C.  Enumeration
    D.  Exposition
        1.
        2.
        3.

II. Proof

    A.  Proof 1
        1. support for proof 1
        2. support for proof 1
        3. support for proof 1

    B.  Proof 2
        1. support for proof 2
        2. support for proof 2
        3. support for proof 2

    C.  Proof 3
        1. support for proof 3
        2. support for proof 3
        3. support for proof 3

III. Conclusion

    A.  Thesis
    B.  Summary of Proof
        1.
        2.
        3.

# Type A: From "Cinderella"

**Thesis:**
Cinderella should have gone to the celebration.

**Ask three questions.**
How would you respond to a king's invitation?
Is it rude to stay home when you are invited to go somewhere?
What is the rarest opportunity you have received?

**List two things you can challenge your readers to do that will arouse their attention.**
Seize opportunity while it lasts.
Think about what you would miss if you never left your home.

**Provide a quotation relevant to the issue.**
Source: Revelation 3:20
Quote: "Behold, I stand at the door and knock."

**Exordium**
Challenge: Seize opportunity while it lasts.

# Basic Outline

I. Introduction
    **A. Exordium: challenge on seizing opportunity**
    B. Thesis: Cinderella should have gone to the celebration
    C. Enumeration: for three reasons
    D. Exposition
        1. Marriage
        2. Permission
        3. Family

II. Proof
    A. Marriage
        1. All beautiful girls, king invited
        2. No husband
        3. Prince chose
    B. Permission
        1. Stepmother promised
        2. Birds gave dress
        3. Birds helped
    C. Family
        1. Stepmother cruel
        2. Stepsisters wicked
        3. Not loved by father

III. Conclusion
    A. Thesis: Cinderella should have gone to the celebration
    B. Summary of Proof
        1. Marriage
        2. Permission
        3. Family

Type B: From *The Wind in the Willows*

**Thesis:**
Mole should have left his home.

**Ask three questions.**
Have you ever felt the urge to get out of the house?
What adventures have you experienced?
Do you get tired of cleaning?

**List two things you can challenge your readers to do that will arouse their attention.**
Enjoy the sun while it is out.
Imagine a beautiful day that you are unable to see because you are locked up in the house.

**Provide a quotation relevant to the issue.**
Source: *The Wind in the Willows*, chapter 1
Quote: "Something up above was calling him imperiously, and he made for the steep little tunnel. . ."

**Exordium**
Quote: "Something up above was calling him imperiously, and he made for the steep little tunnel. . ."

# Basic Outline

I. Introduction
   **A. Exordium: quotation from chapter 1**
   B. Thesis: Mole should have left his home
   C. Enumeration: for three reasons
   D. Exposition
      1. New spring
      2. New Friends
      3. New adventures

II. Proof
   A. Spring
      1. Sensed something calling
      2. Enjoy spring
      3. Experience the world above
   B. Friends
      1. Alone
      2. Met Ratty
      3. To meet Badger
   C. New Adventures
      1. To lunch at Toad Hall
      2. To go on a road trip with Ratty and Toad
      3. To help Toad save his home

III. Conclusion
   A. Thesis: Mole should have left his home
   B. Summary of Proof
      1. New spring
      2. New Friends
      3. New Adventures

# Type C: From *Julius Caesar*

**Thesis:**
Brutus should not have stabbed Caesar.

**Ask three questions.**
What kind of man betrays his friends?
Was Caesar Brutus' friend?
Will killing Caesar bring peace?

**List two things you can challenge your readers to do that will arouse their attention.**
Defend the innocent.
Imagine betraying someone close to you.

**Provide a quotation relevant to the issue.**
Source: Marcus Tullius Cicero
Quote: "Nothing is more noble, nothing more venerable than fidelity."

**Exordium**
Question: What kind of man betrays his friends?

# Basic Outline

I. Introduction
    **A. Exordium: question on betraying friends**
    B. Thesis: Brutus should not have stabbed Caesar
    C. Enumeration: for three reasons
    D. Exposition
        1. Brutus
        2. Caesar
        3. Senate

II. Proof
    A. Brutus
        1. Caesar trusted
        2. Caesar's friend
        3. Respected leader of Rome
    B. Caesar
        1. A hero
        2. The people supported
        3. Denied the crown
    C. Senate
        1. All did not join the conspiracy
        2. No vote
        3. Many not aware of plot

III. Conclusion
    A. Thesis: Brutus should not have stabbed Caesar
    B. Summary of Proof
        1. Brutus
        2. Caesar
        3. Senate

# **ESSAY FOUR ARRANGEMENT: AMPLIFICATION**

I. Introduction

    A. Exordium
    B. Thesis
    C. Enumeration
    D. Exposition
        1.
        2.
        3.

II. Proof

    A. Proof 1
        1. support for proof 1
        2. support for proof 1
        3. support for proof 1

    B. Proof 2
        1. support for proof 2
        2. support for proof 2
        3. support for proof 2

    C. Proof 3
        1. support for proof 3
        2. support for proof 3
        3. support for proof 3

III. Conclusion

    A. Thesis
    B. Summary of Proof
        1.
        2.
        3.
    **C. Amplification**
        **1. To whom it matters**
        **2. Why it matters**

# Type A: From "Cinderella"

**Thesis:**
Cinderella should have gone to the celebration.

**Identify the audience.**
Cinderella
Prince, birds, her family

**Select groups or a person this audience cares about.**
Cinderella: mother and family
Prince: future wife

**Explain why the audience cares.**
The prince falls in love with Cinderella and wants to marry her

**Express this idea as an amplification.**
By going to the celebration, Cinderella meets the prince who falls in love with her and wants to make her his wife.

# Basic Outline

I. Introduction
    A. Exordium: challenge on seizing opportunity
    B. Thesis: Cinderella should have gone to the celebration
    C. Enumeration: for three reasons
    D. Exposition
        1. Marriage
        2. Permission
        3. Family

II. Proof
    A. Marriage
        1. All beautiful girls, king invited
        2. No husband
        3. Prince chose
    B. Permission
        1. Stepmother promised
        2. Birds gave dress
        3. Birds helped
    C. Family
        1. Stepmother cruel
        2. Stepsisters wicked
        3. Not loved by father

III. Conclusion
    A. Thesis: Cinderella should have gone to the celebration
    B. Summary of Proof
        1. Marriage
        2. Permission
        3. Family
    **C. Amplification**
        **1. To whom it matters: prince**
        **2. Why it matters: falls in love with future wife**

Type B: From *The Wind in the Willows*

**Thesis:**
Mole should have left his home.

**Identify the audience.**
Mole
Animals, Ratty, Badger, Toad, parents, youth, friends

**Select groups or a person this audience cares about.**
Mole: friends
Toad: himself and his stuff, friends

**Explain why the audience cares.**
Leaving home led Mole to discover new friends whom he was able to help

**Express this idea as an amplification.**
By leaving home, Mole learned how to make new friends whom he cared about and was able to help when they fell into trouble.

# Basic Outline

I. Introduction
   A. Exordium: quote from chapter 1
   B. Thesis: Mole should have left his home
   C. Enumeration: for three reasons
   D. Exposition
      1. New spring
      2. New Friends
      3. New adventures

II. Proof
   A. Spring
      1. Sensed something calling
      2. Enjoy spring
      3. Experience the world above
   B. Friends
      1. Alone
      2. Met Ratty
      3. To meet Badger
   C. New Adventures
      1. To lunch at Toad Hall
      2. To go on a road trip with Ratty and Toad
      3. To help Toad save his home

III. Conclusion
   A. Thesis: Mole should have left his home
   B. Summary of Proof
      1. New spring
      2. New Friends
      3. New Adventures
   **C. Amplification**
      **1. To whom it matters: Mole**
      **2. Why it matters: help friends**

# Type C: From *Julius Caesar*

**Thesis:**
Brutus should not have stabbed Caesar.

**Identify the audience.**
Brutus
Roman citizens, senators, the families of Brutus and Caesar

**Select groups or a person this audience cares about.**
Brutus: Caesar
Roman citizens: Caesar, Rome, general population

**Explain why the audience cares.**
They love Caesar for his favor which he has bestowed upon them

**Express this idea as an amplification.**
The fanned rage of the Roman citizens sparked by Caesar's death will turn upon the murderous ban of guilty senators.

# Basic Outline

I. Introduction
    A. Exordium: question on betraying friends
    B. Thesis: Brutus should not have stabbed Caesar
    C. Enumeration: for three reasons
    D. Exposition
        1. Brutus trusted
        2. Caesar loved
        3. Senate divided

II. Proof
    A. Brutus trusted
        1. Caesar trusted
        2. Caesar's friend
        3. Respected leader of Rome
    B. Caesar loved
        1. A hero
        2. The people supported
        3. Denied the crown
    C. Senate divided
        1. All did not join the conspiracy
        2. No vote
        3. Many not aware of plot

III. Conclusion
    A. Thesis: Brutus should not have stabbed Caesar
    B. Summary of Proof
        1. Brutus trusted
        2. Caesar loved
        3. Senate divided
    **C. Amplification**
        **1. To whom it matters: Roman citizens**
        **2. Why it matters: love for Caesar's good will toward them**

# **ESSAY FIVE ARRANGEMENT: DIVISION**

I. Introduction
   A. Exordium
   **B. Division**
       **1. Agreement**
       **2. Disagreement**
           **a. Thesis**
           **b. Counter-Thesis**
   C. Distribution
       1. Thesis
       2. Enumeration
       3. Exposition
           a.
           b.
           c.

II. Proof
   A. Proof 1
       1.
       2.
       3.
   B. Proof 2
       1.
       2.
       3.
   C. Proof 3
       1.
       2.
       3.

III. Conclusion
   A. Thesis
   B. Summary of Proof
       1.
       2.
       3.
   C. Amplification
       1. To whom it matters
       2. Why it matters

Type A: From "Cinderella"

**Thesis:**
Cinderella should have gone to the celebration.

**Counter-Thesis:**
Cinderella should not have gone to the celebration.

**Common Terms:**
Cinderella, celebration

**Common Opinion:**
Both sides agree: Cinderella is invited, the prince is at the celebration
Both sides want: to marry the prince

**Choose one point of common agreement.**
Cinderella is invited to the celebration

**Some people believe . . . (Thesis)**
Cinderella should have gone to the celebration

**Conversely, others believe that . . . (Counter-Thesis)**
Cinderella should not have gone to the celebration

**Division:**
Everyone agrees that Cinderella is invited to the celebration, but some believe that Cinderella should have gone to the celebration and some believe that she should not have gone to the celebration.

# Basic Outline

I. Introduction
    A. Exordium: challenge on seizing opportunity
    **B. Division**
        **1. Agreement: Cinderella invited to the celebration**
        **2. Disagreement**
           **a. Cinderella should have gone to the celebration**
           **b. Cinderella should not have gone to the celebration**
    C. Distribution
        1. Thesis: Cinderella should have gone to the celebration
        2. Enumeration: for three reasons
        3. Exposition
           a. Marriage
           b. Permission
           c. Family

II. Proof
    A. Marriage
        1. All beautiful girls, king invited
        2. No husband
        3. Prince chose
    B. Permission
        1. Stepmother promised
        2. Birds gave dress
        3. Birds helped
    C. Family
        1. Stepmother cruel
        2. Stepsisters wicked
        3. Not loved by father

III. Conclusion
    A. Thesis: Cinderella should have gone to the celebration
    B. Summary of Proof
        1. Marriage
        2. Permission
        3. Family
    C. Amplification
        1. To whom it matters: prince
        2. Why it matters: falls in love with future wife

# Type B: From *The Wind in the Willows*

**Thesis:**
Mole should have left his home.

**Counter-Thesis:**
Mole should not have left his home.

**Common Terms:**
Mole, home

**Common Opinion:**
Both sides agree: a home provides comfort and protection, Mole is restless
Both sides want: a place to call home

**Choose one point of common agreement.**
A home provides comfort and protection

**Some people believe . . . (Thesis)**
Mole should have left his home.

**Conversely, others believe that . . . (Counter-Thesis)**
Mole should not have left his home.

**Division:**
Everyone agrees that a home provides comfort and protection, but some believe that Mole should have left his home and some believe that he should not have left his home.

# Basic Outline III

I. Introduction
   A. Exordium: quote from chapter 1
   **B. Division**
      **1. Agreement: A home comfort and protection**
      **2. Disagreement**
         **a. Mole should have left his home**
         **b. Mole should not have left his home**
   C. Distribution
      1. Thesis: Mole should have left his home
      2. Enumeration: for three reasons
      3. Exposition
         a. New spring
         b. New Friends
         c. New adventures

II. Proof
   A. Spring
      1. Sensed something calling
      2. Enjoy spring
      3. Experience the world above
   B. Friends
      1. Alone
      2. Met Ratty
      3. To meet Badger
   C. New Adventures
      1. To lunch at Toad Hall
      2. To go on a road trip with Ratty and Toad
      3. To help Toad save his home

III. Conclusion
   A. Thesis: Mole should have left his home
   B. Summary of Proof
      1. New spring
      2. New Friends
      3. New Adventures
   C. Amplification
      1. To whom it matters: Mole
      2. Why it matters: to help friends

## Type C: From *Julius Caesar*

**Thesis:**
Brutus should not have stabbed Caesar.

**Counter-Thesis:**
Brutus should have stabbed Caesar.

**Common Terms:**
Brutus, stabbed, Caesar

**Common Opinion:**
Both sides agree: Caesar is an important leader
Both sides want: what is best for Rome

**Choose one point of common agreement.**
Caesar is an important leader

**Some people believe . . . (Thesis)**
Brutus should not have stabbed Caesar.

**Conversely, others believe that . . . (Counter-Thesis)**
Brutus should have stabbed Caesar.

**Division:**
Every Roman agrees that Caesar is an important leader, but some believe that Brutus should not have stabbed Caesar and some believe that he should have stabbed Caesar.

# Basic Outline

I. Introduction
   A. Exordium: question on betraying friends
   **B. Division**
      **1. Agreement: Caesar important leader**
      **2. Disagreement**
         **a. Brutus should not have stabbed Caesar**
         **b. Brutus should have stabbed Caesar**
   C. Distribution
      1. Thesis: Brutus should not have stabbed Caesar
      2. Enumeration: for three reasons
      3. Exposition
         a. Brutus trusted
         b. Caesar loved
         c. Senate divided

II. Proof
   A. Brutus trusted
      1. Caesar trusted
      2. Caesar's friend
      3. Respected leader of Rome
   B. Caesar loved
      1. A hero
      2. The people supported
      3. Denied the crown
   C. Senate divided
      1. All did not join the conspiracy
      2. No vote
      3. Many not aware of plot

III. Conclusion
   A. Thesis: Brutus should not have stabbed Caesar
   B. Summary of Proof
      1. Brutus trusted
      2. Caesar loved
      3. Senate divided
   C. Amplification
      1. To whom it matters: Roman citizens
      2. Why it matters: love for Caesar's good will toward them

# *ESSAY SIX ARRANGEMENT: REFUTATION*

I. Introduction
   A. Exordium
   B. Division
       1. Agreement
       2. Disagreement
          a. Thesis
          b. Counter-Thesis
   C. Distribution
       1. Thesis
       2. Enumeration
       3. Exposition
          a.
          b.
          c.

II. Proof
   A. Proof 1
       1.
       2.
       3.
   B. Proof 2
       1.
       2.
       3.
   C. Proof 3
       1.
       2.
       3.

III. **Refutation**
   **A. Counter-Thesis**
   **B. Counter-Proof 1**
       **1. Summary of support for reason 1**
       **2. Inadequacy of reason 1**
   **C. Counter-Proof 2**
       **1. Summary of support for reason 2**
       **2. Inadequacy of reason 2**
   **D. Summary of Refutation**

IV. Conclusion
   A. Thesis
   B. Summary of Proof
       1.
       2.
       3.
   C. Amplification
       1. To whom it matters
       2. Why it matters

# Type A: From "Cinderella"

**Thesis:**
Cinderella should have gone to the celebration.

**Counter-thesis:**
Cinderella should not have gone to the celebration.

**Counter-Proof 1:** Needs to follow instructions
1. Stepmom told her to stay home
2. Needs to obey her parents
3. Mother told her to be good

**Explain why this proof is not persuasive.**
Cinderella was unfairly prohibited from attending the celebration by her stepmother who despised her. Her stepmother had no just reason for keeping Cinderella at home.

**Counter-Proof 2:** Cinderella was not ready to go to the celebration
1. She did not have a dress
2. She did not pick the lentils
3. She did not know how to dance

**Explain why this proof is not persuasive.**
Even though Cinderella was not ready to attend the celebration, she received help from the birds who lived in the tree at her mother's grave. After receiving their help, Cinderella was ready to attend the celebration.

**Summary of Refutation:**
Neither the need to follow instructions nor Cinderella's unpreparedness for attending the celebration provides sufficient reason for prohibiting Cinderella from going to the celebration.

# Basic Outline

I. Introduction
   A. Exordium: challenge on seizing opportunity
   B. Division
      1. Agreement: Cinderella invited
      2. Disagreement
         a. Cinderella should have gone to the celebration
         b. Cinderella should not have gone to the celebration
   C. Distribution
      1. Thesis: Cinderella should have gone to the celebration
      2. Enumeration: for three reasons
      3. Exposition
         a. Marriage
         b. Permission
         c. Family

II. Proof
   A. Marriage
      1. All beautiful girls, king invited
      2. No husband
      3. Prince chose
   B. Permission
      1. Stepmother promised
      2. Birds gave dress
      3. Birds helped
   C. Family
      1. Stepmother cruel
      2. Stepsisters wicked
      3. Not loved by father

**III. Refutation**
   **A. Counter-Thesis: Cinderella should not have gone to the celebration**
   **B. Counter-Proof 1: Needs to follow instructions**
      **1. Summary of support for reason 1: stepmom, obey parents, mother**
      **2. Inadequacy of reason 1: unfairly prohibited**
   **C. Counter-Proof 2: Not ready to attend celebration**
      **1. Summary of support for reason 2: dress, lentils, dance**
      **2. Inadequacy of reason 2: help from the birds**
   **D. Summary of Refutation: insufficient reason to prohibit Cinderella**

III. Conclusion
   A. Thesis: Cinderella should have gone to the celebration
   B. Summary of Proof
      1. Marriage
      2. Permission
      3. Family
   C. Amplification
      1. To whom it matters: prince
      2. Why it matters: falls in love with future wife

## Type B: From *The Wind in the Willows*

**Thesis:**
Mole should have left his home.

**Counter-thesis:**
Mole should not have left his home.

**Counter-Proof 1:** It is too dangerous
    1. Mole fell into the river
    2. He gets lost in the Wild Wood
    3. Someone could take his home

**Explain why this proof is not persuasive.**
The possibility of danger does not make danger certain. Because something might happen does not mean that it will happen.

**Counter-Proof 2:** Mole is too impatient
    1. He is not done cleaning his house
    2. His home is safe
    3. He is easily distracted

**Explain why this proof is not persuasive.**
Mole's impatience actually gives him more reason to leave his home for fresh air and a change.

**Summary of Refutation:**
Neither the possibility of danger nor Mole's impatience provides sufficient reason for Mole to have stayed home.

# Basic Outline

I. Introduction
   A. Exordium: quotation from chapter 1
   B. Division
       1. Agreement: A home comfort and protection
       2. Disagreement
          a. Mole should have left his home
          b. Mole should not have left his home
   C. Distribution
       1. Thesis: Mole should have left his home
       2. Enumeration: for three reasons
       3. Exposition
          a. New spring
          b. New Friends
          c. New adventures

II. Proof
   A. Spring
       1. Sensed something calling
       2. Enjoy spring
       3. Experience the world above
   B. Friends
       1. Alone
       2. Met Ratty
       3. To meet Badger
   C. New Adventures
       1. To lunch at Toad Hall
       2. To go on a road trip with Ratty and Toad
       3. To help Toad save his home

III. **Refutation**
   **A. Counter-Thesis: Mole should not have left his home**
   **B. Counter-Proof 1: Too dangerous**
       **1. Summary of support for reason 1: river, Wild Wood, lose home**
       **2. Inadequacy of reason 1: possibility is not certainty**
   **C. Counter-Proof 2: Mole impatient**
       **1. Summary of support for reason 2: still cleaning, safe, distracted**
       **2. Inadequacy of reason 2: reasons to leave not stay home**
   **D. Summary of Refutation: insufficient reason to stay home**

IV. Conclusion
   A. Thesis: Mole should have left his home
   B. Summary of Proof
       1. New spring
       2. New Friends
       3. New Adventures
   C. Amplification
       1. To whom it matters: Mole
       2. Why it matters: to help his friends

# Type C: From *Julius Caesar*

**Thesis:**
Brutus should not have stabbed Caesar.

**Counter-thesis:**
Brutus should have stabbed Caesar.

**Counter-Proof 1:** Caesar's lust for power
 1. Caesar threatened Rome's freedom
 2. Caesar was ambitious
 3. Caesar brought his army into Rome

**Explain why this proof is not persuasive.**
Caesar's lust for power required political action, not military. Brutus turned the Senate floor into a battlefield.

**Counter-Proof 2:** Brutus' love for Rome
 1. Caesar threatened Rome's freedom
 2. To preserve liberty
 3. Brutus loved Rome more

**Explain why this proof is not persuasive.**
Caesar loved Rome no less than Brutus. The notion that Caesar threatened the liberty of Rome lacked sufficient evidence and emerged more from the irrational fears of a few men than the temperate love of the multitude.

**Summary of Refutation:**
Neither the argument that Caesar intended to use his military strength to enslave Rome nor the argument that Brutus acted out of a greater love than Caesar for the good of Rome provides sufficient reason for assassinating a man loved by those whom he served to protect.

# Basic Outline

I. Introduction
    A. Exordium: question on betraying friends
    B. Division
        1. Agreement: Caesar important leader
        2. Disagreement
            a. Brutus should not have stabbed Caesar
            b. Brutus should have stabbed Caesar
    C. Distribution
        1. Thesis: Brutus should not have stabbed Caesar
        2. Enumeration: for three reasons
        3. Exposition
            a. Brutus trusted
            b. Caesar loved
            c. Senate divided

II. Proof
    A. Brutus trusted
        1. Caesar trusted
        2. Caesar's friend
        3. Respected leader of Rome
    B. Caesar loved
        1. A hero
        2. The people supported
        3. Denied the crown
    C. Senate divided
        1. All did not join the conspiracy
        2. No vote
        3. Many not aware of plot

III. **Refutation**
    **A. Counter-Thesis: Brutus should have stabbed Caesar.**
    **B. Counter-Proof 1: Caesar's lust for power**
        **1. Summary: Threat to freedom; ambition; army in Rome**
        **2. Inadequacy: Rome a city not a battlefield**
    **C. Counter-Proof 2: Brutus' love for Rome**
        **1. Summary: Freedom; liberty; greater love for Rome**
        **2. Inadequacy: Loved Rome no less than Brutus**
    **D. Summary of Refutation: insufficient reason to assassinate a beloved leader**

IV. Conclusion
    A. Thesis: Brutus should not have stabbed Caesar
    B. Summary of Proof
        1. Brutus trusted
        2. Caesar loved
        3. Senate divided
    C. Amplification
        1. To whom it matters: Roman citizens
        2. Why it matters: love for Caesar's good will toward them

# ESSAY SEVEN ARRANGEMENT: NARRATIVE

I. Introduction
   A. Exordium
   **B. Narratio**
      **1. Situation**
      **2. Actions**
   C. Division
      1. Agreement
      2. Disagreement
         a. Thesis
         b. Counter-Thesis
   D. Distribution
      1. Thesis
      2. Enumeration
      3. Exposition
         a.
         b.
         c.

II. Proof
   A. Proof 1
      1.
      2.
      3.
   B. Proof 2
      1.
      2.
      3.
   C. Proof 3
      1.
      2.
      3.

III. Refutation
   A. Counter-Thesis
   B. Counter-Proof 1
      1. Summary of support for reason 1
      2. Inadequacy of reason 1
   C. Counter-Proof 2
      1. Summary of support for reason 2
      2. Inadequacy of reason 2
   D. Summary of Refutation

IV. Conclusion
   A. Thesis
   B. Summary of Proof
      1.
      2.
      3.
   C. Amplification
      1. To whom it matters
      2. Why it matters

# Type A: From "Cinderella"

**Thesis:**
Cinderella should have gone to the celebration.

**What is the situation of the issue?**
Time: Spring after mother's death
Place: Kingdom, king's palace
Actors: Cinderella, stepmother, stepsisters, prince
Dilemma: Cinderella wanted to go to the celebration

**What action or event caused this situation?**
Stepmother told her that she could not go

**What caused the action above? List a sequence of causes that led to this situation.**
Birds help Cinderella pick lentils out of the ashes
Cinderella must pick lentils out of the ashes
Cinderella asked stepmother if she could go to the celebration
King invited all the beautiful girls in the kingdom

**Decide what to include in the narratio and order the events.**
Situation: spring, Cinderella want to go to the celebration at the king's palace
Stepmother told her that she could not go
Cinderella asked stepmother if she could go to the celebration
King invited all the beautiful girls in the kingdom

**Narratio:**
One spring the king wanted to find a wife for his son so he invited all of the beautiful girls in the kingdom to attend a three-day celebration. Cinderella asked her stepmother if she could go, but her stepmother told her that she was dirty, did not have a dress, and could not dance. After she begged to go, the stepmother dumped a bowl of lentils in a pile of ashes and said that she could go if all the lentils were cleaned in one hour. When Cinderella finish the task, her stepmother repeated that Cinderella could not go to the celebration.

# Persuasive Outline

I. Introduction
   A. Exordium: challenge on seizing opportunity
   **B. Narratio**
      **1. Situation: spring, celebration at king's palace**
      **2. Actions: invitation to celebration, stepmother denied**
   C. Division
      1. Agreement: Cinderella invited
      2. Disagreement
         a. Cinderella should have gone to the celebration
         b. Cinderella should not have gone to the celebration
   C. Distribution
      1. Thesis: Cinderella should have gone to the celebration
      2. Enumeration: for three reasons
      3. Exposition
         a. Marriage
         b. Permission
         c. Family

II. Proof
   A. Marriage
      1. All beautiful girls, king invited
      2. No husband
      3. Prince chose
   B. Permission
      1. Stepmother promised
      2. Birds gave dress
      3. Birds helped
   C. Family
      1. Stepmother cruel
      2. Stepsisters wicked
      3. Not loved by father

III. Refutation
   A. Counter-Thesis: Cinderella should not have gone to the celebration
   B. Counter-Proof 1: Needs to follow instructions
      1. Summary of support for reason 1: stepmom, obey parents, mother
      2. Inadequacy of reason 1: unfairly prohibited
   C. Counter-Proof 2: Not ready to attend celebration
      1. Summary of support for reason 2: dress, lentils, dance
      2. Inadequacy of reason 2: help from the birds
   D. Summary of Refutation: insufficient reason to prohibit Cinderella

III. Conclusion
   A. Thesis: Cinderella should have gone to the celebration
   B. Summary of Proof
      1. Marriage
      2. Permission
      3. Family
   C. Amplification
      1. To whom it matters: prince
      2. Why it matters: falls in love with future wife

Type B: From *The Wind in the Willows*

**Thesis:**
Mole should have left his home.

**What is the situation of the issue?**
Time: Spring
Place: Mole's home underground
Actors: Mole
Dilemma: Mole feels an urge to leave home

**What action or event caused this situation?**
Spring has arrived

**What caused the action above? List a sequence of causes that led to this situation.**
Spring was moving through the air above and below the ground
Mole began cleaning his home
It was morning
Winter ended

**Decide what to include in the narratio and order the events.**
Situation: spring, Mole cleaning his home underground
Spring was moving through the air above and below the ground
Mole began cleaning his home
Winter ended

**Narratio:**
Now that winter had ended, spring was moving through the air above and below the ground. Mole woke up one morning and began cleaning his home. As he cleaned, he felt something calling him to leave what he was doing and climb up out of his hole.

# Persuasive Outline

I. Introduction
   A. Exordium: quote from chapter 1
   **B. Narratio**
      **1. Situation: spring, Mole cleaning his home underground**
      **2. Actions: winter ended, Mole cleaning, spring moving**
   C. Division
      1. Agreement: A home comfort and protection
      2. Disagreement
          a. Mole should have left his home
          b. Mole should not have left his home
   D. Distribution
      1. Thesis: Mole should have left his home
      2. Enumeration: for three reasons
      3. Exposition
          a. New spring
          b. New Friends
          c. New adventures

II. Proof
   A. Spring
      1. Sensed something calling
      2. Enjoy spring
      3. Experience the world above
   B. Friends
      1. Alone
      2. Met Ratty
      3. To meet Badger
   C. New Adventures
      1. To lunch at Toad Hall
      2. To go on a road trip with Ratty and Toad
      3. To help Toad save his home

III. Refutation
   A. Counter-Thesis: Mole should not have left his home
   B. Counter-Proof 1: It is too dangerous
      1. Summary of support for reason 1: river, Wild Wood, lose home
      2. Inadequacy of reason 1: possibility is not certainty
   C. Counter-Proof 2: Mole is impatient
      1. Summary of support for reason 2: still cleaning, safe, distracted
      2. Inadequacy of reason 2: reasons to leave not stay home
   D. Summary of Refutation: insufficient reason to stay home

IV. Conclusion
   A. Thesis: Mole should have left his home
   B. Summary of Proof
      1. New spring
      2. New Friends
      3. New Adventures
   C. Amplification
      1. To whom it matters: Mole
      2. Why it matters: to help friends

# Type C: From *Julius Caesar*

**Thesis:**
Brutus should not have stabbed Caesar.

**What is the situation of the issue?**
Time: Ides of March, 43 B.C., day
Place: City of Rome, Senate
Actors: Caesar, Cassius, Brutus, Senate, people of Rome
Dilemma: Brutus does not want to lose the Republic

**What action or event caused this situation?**
Caesar goes before the Senate to receive a crown as emperor

**What caused the action above? List a sequence of causes that led to this situation.**
Cassius secretly met with Brutus to gain his support for a conspiracy to kill Caesar
Some senators fear Caesar, tyranny, and the loss of freedom
Caesar denied the crown during the games
People celebrated in the streets
Caesar returned to Rome bringing his army with him into the city

**Decide what to include in the narratio and order the events.**
Situation: Rome, Ides of March, Brutus does not want to lose the Republic
Cassius secretly met with Brutus to gain his support for a conspiracy to kill Caesar
Some senators fear Caesar, tyranny, and the loss of freedom
People celebrated in the streets
Caesar returned to Rome bringing his army with him into the city

**Narratio:**
Having completed his military campaigns with success, Caesar makes a bold move by returning to Rome and bringing his army with him. While Roman officials fear the possible outcome of Caesar's return, the people have crowded the streets to celebrate his recent arrival. Meanwhile, Cassius has been plotting with other senators to assassinate Caesar before he is crowned emperor. He needs to persuade one other senator, Brutus, to join their conspiracy. Cassius first unveils the senators' plan to Brutus in the streets during Caesar's grand entry. Though at first not favorable to the plan, Brutus is eventually won over by Cassius' persistent counsel.

# Persuasive Outline

I. Introduction
    A. Exordium: question on betraying friends
    **B. Narratio**
        **1. Situation: Rome, Ides of March, lose Republic**
        **2. Actions: Caesar's return, celebration, conspiracy plot**
    C. Division
        1. Agreement: Caesar important leader
        2. Disagreement
            a. Brutus should not have stabbed Caesar
            b. Brutus should have stabbed Caesar
    D. Distribution
        1. Thesis: Brutus should not have stabbed Caesar
        2. Enumeration: for three reasons
        3. Exposition
            a. Brutus trusted
            b. Caesar loved
            c. Senate divided

IV. Proof
    A. Brutus trusted
        1. Caesar trusted
        2. Caesar's friend
        3. Respected leader of Rome
    B. Caesar loved
        1. A hero
        2. The people supported
        3. Denied the crown
    C. Senate divided
        1. All did not join the conspiracy
        2. No vote
        3. Many not aware of plot

III. Refutation
    A. Counter-Thesis: Brutus should have stabbed Caesar.
    B. Counter-Proof 1: Caesar's lust for power
        1. Summary: Threat to freedom; ambition; army in Rome
        2. Inadequacy: Rome a city not a battlefield
    C. Counter-Proof 2: Brutus' love for Rome
        1. Summary: Freedom; liberty; greater love for Rome
        2. Inadequacy: Loved Rome no less than Brutus
    D. Summary of Refutation: insufficient reason to assassinate a beloved leader

IV. Conclusion
    A. Thesis: Brutus should not have stabbed Caesar
    B. Summary of Proof
        1. Brutus trusted
        2. Caesar loved
        3. Senate divided
    C. Amplification
        1. To whom it matters: Roman citizens
        2. Why it matters: love for Caesar's good will toward them

# **_ESSAY EIGHT ARRANGEMENT: REVIEW_**

I. Introduction
   A. Exordium
   B. Narratio
      1. Situation
      2. Actions
   C. Division
      1. Agreement
      2. Disagreement
         a. Thesis
         b. Counter-Thesis
   D. Distribution
      1. Thesis
      2. Enumeration
      3. Exposition
         a.
         b.
         c.

II. Proof
   A. Proof 1
      1.
      2.
      3.
   B. Proof 2
      1.
      2.
      3.
   C. Proof 3
      1.
      2.
      3.

III. Refutation
   A. Counter-Thesis
   B. Counter-Proof 1
      1. Summary of support for reason 1
      2. Inadequacy of reason 1
   C. Counter-Proof 2
      1. Summary of support for reason 2
      2. Inadequacy of reason 2
   D. Summary of Refutation

IV. Conclusion
   A. Thesis
   B. Summary of Proof
      1.
      2.
      3.
   C. Amplification
      1. To whom it matters
      2. Why it matters

# Part Three
# **Elocution**

# ESSAY ONE ELOCUTION: OUTLINE TO ESSAY

## Type A: From "Cinderella"

Cinderella should have gone to the celebration for three reasons: The king invited all the beautiful girls in the kingdom, her stepmother promised she could go, and she does not have a husband.

The first reason Cinderella should have gone to the celebration is that the king invited all the beautiful girls in the kingdom. The second reason Cinderella should have gone to the celebration is that her stepmother promised she could go. The third reason Cinderella should have gone to the celebration is that she does not have a husband.

Cinderella should have gone to the celebration because the king invited all the beautiful girls in the kingdom, her stepmother promised she could go, and she does not have a husband.

## Type B: From *The Wind in the Willows*

Mole should have left his home for three reasons: He was alone, he did not like spring cleaning, and he met new friends.

The first reason Mole should have left his home is that he was alone. The second reason Mole should have left his home is that he did not like spring cleaning. The third reason Mole should have left his home is that he met new friends.

Mole should have left his home because he was alone, he did not like spring cleaning, and he met new friends.

## Type B: From *The Wind in the Willows*

Brutus should not have stabbed Caesar for three reasons: Caesar trusted Brutus, the people supported Caesar, and Brutus was a respected leader of Rome.

The first reason Brutus should not have stabbed Caesar is that Caesar trusted Brutus. The second reason Brutus should not have stabbed Caesar is that the people supported Caesar. The third reason Brutus should not have stabbed Caesar is that Brutus was a respected leader of Rome.

Brutus should not have stabbed Caesar because Caesar trusted Brutus, the people supported Caesar, and Brutus was a respected leader of Rome.

# *ESSAY TWO ELOCUTION: PARALLELISM I*

From *Grimms' Tales for Young and Old*, translated by Ralph Manheim

From then on she had to do all the work, getting up before daybreak, **carrying water, lighting fires, cooking, and washing**.

So he bought beautiful **dresses, diamonds, and pearls** for his two step-daughters, and on the way home, as he was riding through a copse, a hazel branch brushed against him and knocked off his hat.

From Grahame's *The Wind in the Willows*

Hither and thither through the meadows he rambled busily, . . . everything **happy**, and **progressive**, and **occupied**.

There's real life for you, embodied in that little cart. The open road, the dusty highway, the **heath**, the **common**, the **hedgerows**, the **rolling downs**!

Then a short, quick run forward—a **fault**—a **check**—a **try** back; and then a **slow, steady, confident** advance.

From Shakespeare's *Julius Caesar*

Act 2, Scene 1
'**Speak, strike, redress!**' Am I entreated to speak, and strike? O Rome! I make thee promise;

For he is superstitious grown of late, quite from the main opinion he held once of **fantasy**, of **dreams**, and **ceremonies**.

Act 2, Scene 2
Your statue spouting blood in many pipes, in which so many smiling Romans bath'd, signifies that from you great Rome shall suck reviving blood, and that great men shall press for **tinctures, stains, relics, and cognizance**.

Act 3, Scene 1
Some to the common pulpits, and cry out, '**Liberty, freedom, and enfranchisement!**'

Act 3, Scene 2
**Friends, Romans, countrymen**, lend me your ears;

## Type A: From "Cinderella"

Essay Two Parallelism Edits

**Term**
Cinderella

| | |
|---|---|
| **Nouns**<br>father, prince, stepmother, stepsisters | **Parallel structures**<br><br>Cinderella lived with her **father, stepmother, and stepsisters**. |
| **Verbs**<br>cry, clean, sleep, dance, run, hide, ask, pray, work | Everyday Cinderella **cleaned, worked,** and **slept** in the ashes. |
| **Adjectives**<br>dirty, sad, kind, obedient, faithful | The **kind, obedient, and faithful** Cinderella should have gone to the celebration. |
| **Adverbs**<br>quickly, respectfully, mournfully | Cinderella **quickly, respectfully, and mournfully** did her chores. |

## Type B: From *The Wind in the Willows*

Essay Two Parallelism Edits

**Term**
Home

| | |
|---|---|
| **Nouns**<br>river, wood, meadow | **Parallel structures**<br><br>Mole left his home to experience the **river**, the **woods**, and the **meadows**. |
| **Verbs**<br>protect, comfort, relax | Mole's home **relaxes, comforts,** and **protects** him. |
| **Adjectives**<br>safe, comfortable, peaceful | Mole should have left his **safe, comfortable, and peaceful** home. |
| **Adverbs**<br>firmly, comfortably, peacefully | Mole's home remained **firmly, comfortably, and peacefully** secure. |

# Type C: From *Julius Caesar*

<u>Essay Two Parallelism Edits</u>

**Term**
Brutus

**Nouns**
Cassius, Caesar, Senate, Casca, Antony

**Verbs**
leads, thinks, examines, listens

**Adjectives**
honorable, respectable, careful

**Adverbs**
slowly, thoughtfully, cautiously

**Parallel structures**

**Brutus, Cassius, and Casca** are senators.

Brutus should **listen, examine,** and **think** about the senators' plan.

The **careful, honorable,** and **respectable** Brutus should not have stabbed Caesar.

Brutus considered the plan **slowly, cautiously,** and **thoughtfully**.

# ESSAY THREE ELOCUTION: VERBS

*The types in the left-hand column, below, display verbs that are vague and passive. The sentences can be rewritten using verbs that are precise and active as seen in the right-hand column.*

<u>Vague Verbs</u>

I've **put** a bowlful of lentils in the ashes.

Ashputtle **put** on the dress as fast as she could and went to the wedding.

He thought his happiness was complete when, as he **went** aimlessly along, suddenly he **was** by the edge of a full-fed river.

He **came** to the surface and tried to grasp the reeds and the rushes that **were** along the water's edge close under the bank, but the stream **was** so strong that it took them out of his hands.

I'll **make** the vulgar leave the streets.

Through this the well-beloved Brutus **put** his knife; and, as he **pulled** his cursed steel away, **see** how the blood of Caesar **came** out of it, . . .

<u>Precise Verbs</u>

Here, I've **dumped** a bowlful of lentils in the ashes.

Ashputtle **slipped** into the dress as fast as she could and went to the wedding.

He thought his happiness was complete when, as he **meandered** aimlessly along, suddenly he **stood** by the edge of a full-fed river.

He **rose** to the surface and tried to grasp the reeds and the rushes that **grew** along the water's edge close under the bank, but the stream was so strong that it **tore** them out of his hands.

I'll about and **drive** away the vulgar from the streets.

Through this the well-beloved Brutus **stabbed**; and, as he **plucked** his cursed steel away, **mark** how the blood of Caesar **followed** it, . . .

<u>Passive Verbs</u>

Peas and lentils **were poured** into the ashes by Cinderella's stepsisters.

The tree **was chopped** down by the prince.

Mole **was found** hiding in a hollow.

Toad Hall **was invaded** by the Weasels.

Caesar **was warned** by the Soothsayer to beware the Ides of March.

A thought **was planted** in Brutus' head by Cassius.

<u>Active Verbs</u>

Cinderella's stepsisters **poured** peas and lentils into the ashes.

The prince **chopped** down the tree.

Ratty **found** Mole hiding in a hollow.

The Weasels **invaded** Toad Hall.

As Caesar passed, the Soothsayer **warned** him to beware the Ides of March.

Cassius **planted** a thought in Brutus' head.

# Type A: From "Cinderella"

<u>Essay Three Verbs Edits</u>

She **had** permission. (vague)

Cinderella **did** not yet **have** a husband. (vague)

After she asked, her stepmother **said** Cinderella could **go** to the celebration if she picked all the lentils out of the ashes within an hour. (vague)

After Cinderella **got** all the lentils with the help of the birds, her stepmother changed her mind. (vague)

However, Cinderella **was helped** again by a bird in the hazel tree who **gave** Cinderella a dress for the celebration. (passive, vague)

Her stepmother and stepsisters **were** cruel. (vague)

They **made** fun of Cinderella and mistreated her. (vague)

Cinderella **was** also not **loved** by her father. (passive)

She **received** permission.

Cinderella **had** not yet **married** a young man.

After she asked, her stepmother **promised** that Cinderella could **attend** the celebration if she picked all the lentils out of the ashes within an hour.

After Cinderella **cleaned** all the lentils with the help of the birds, her stepmother changed her mind.

However, another bird **helped** Cinderella when it **tossed** down a dress out of the hazel tree for the celebration.

Her stepmother and stepsisters **abused** her.

They **mocked** Cinderella and mistreated her.

Also, Cinderella's father did not **love** her.

# Type B: From *The Wind in the Willows*

Essay Three Verbs Edits

It **was** spring. (vague)

He could **go** on new adventures. (vague)

He did not **like** spring cleaning and wanted to **go** out of his home to enjoy the spring. (vague)

At home, Mole **was** alone. (vague)

After lunch, he **was persuaded** by Toad to go on a road trip where an automobile ran them off the road and wrecked their cart. (passive)

Mole also helped Toad save his home from the Weasels who **took** Toad Hall while Toad **was** in jail. (vague)

Spring **had arrived.**

He could **experience** new adventures.

He **hated** spring cleaning and wanted to **climb** up out of his home to enjoy the spring.

At home, Mole **lived** alone.

After lunch, Toad **persuaded** Mole to go on a road trip where an automobile ran them off the road and wrecked their cart.

Mole also helped Toad save his home from the Weasels who **invaded** Toad Hall while Toad **served** time in jail.

# Type C: From *Julius Caesar*

## Essay Three Verbs Edits

Brutus **is** trustworthy. (vague)

The Senate **is** not united. (vague)

Not only **was** Brutus **trusted** by Caesar, but the Roman people also looked to Brutus as a respected and trustworthy leader of Rome. (passive)

In fact, they loved him so much that they **wanted to make** him emperor by offering him the crown. (vague)

Many of the senators **were** unaware of the plot and played no part in carrying out this murderous act. (vague)

Such secrecy **kept** a vote off of the Senate floor. (vague)

The people **trusted** Brutus.

The conspirators **acted** in secret.

Not only did Caesar **trust** Brutus, but the Roman people also looked to Brutus as a respected and trustworthy leader of Rome.

In fact, they loved him so much that they desired to **crown** Caesar emperor.

Many of the senators **knew** nothing of the plot and played no part in carrying out this murderous act.

Such secrecy **avoided** the possibility of rejection from opposing senators.

# **ESSAY FOUR ELOCUTION: PARALLELISM II**

From *Grimms' Tales for Young and Old*, translated by Ralph Manheim

Come and help me put the **good ones in the pot**, the **bad ones in your crop**.

They called Ashputtle and said: "**Comb our hair, brush our shoes, and fasten our buckles**."

From Grahame's *The Wind in the Willows*

The **sunshine struck hot on his fur, soft breezes caressed his heated brow**, and after the seclusion of the cellarage he had lived in so long the **carol** of happy birds **fell on his dulled hearing** almost like a shout.

Hither and thither through the meadows he rambled busily, **along the hedgerows, across the copses**, finding everywhere **birds building, flowers budding, leaves thrusting**—everything happy, and progressive, and occupied.

**Eating your grub**, and **drinking your drink**, and **making bad jokes** about you, and **singing vulgar songs**, about—well, about prisons, and magistrates, and policemen; horrid personal songs, with no humour in them.

From Shakespeare's *Julius Caesar*

Act 1, Scene 1
**Run to your houses, fall upon your knees, pray to the gods** to intermit the plague that needs must light on this ingratitude.

Act 2, Scene 1
And, upon my knees, I charm you, **by my once-commended beauty, by all your vows** of love, and **that great vow** which did incorporate and make us one, that you unfold to me, **your self, your half**, why are you heavy, and what men to-night have had resort to you;

Act 2, Scene 3
Caesar, **beware of Brutus; take heed of Cassius; come not near Casca; have an eye to Cinna; trust not Trebonius; mark well Metellus Cimber**; Decius Brutus loves thee not; thou hast wronged Caius Ligarius.

Act 3, Scene 2
There is **tears for his love; joy for his fortune; honour for his valour**; and **death for his ambition**.

When that the **poor have cried, Caesar hath wept**; Ambition should be made of sterner stuff:

## Type A: From "Cinderella"

Essay Four Parallelism Edits

**Phrase or Clause**
she received permission

**Additional phrases or clauses**
she accepted the invitation
she suffered abandonment

**Parallel structures**

Cinderella should have gone to the celebration for three reasons: She **accepted the invitation, received permission,** and **suffered abandonment**.

**Phrase or Clause**
meet the prince and become his bride

**Additional phrases or clauses**
leave her home

She could possibly **meet the prince, become his bride,** and **leave her home**.

## Type B: From *The Wind in the Willows*

Essay Four Parallelism Edits

**Phrase or Clause**
to meet new friends

**Additional phrases or clauses**
to enjoy the new spring
to experience new adventures

**Parallel structures**

Mole should have left his safe, comfortable, and peaceful home for three reasons: He wanted to **enjoy the new spring, to meet new friends,** and **to experience new adventures**.

**Phrase or Clause**
off the road

**Additional phrases or clauses**
into a ditch

After lunch, Toad persuaded Mole to go on a road trip where an automobile ran them **off the road, into a ditch,** and wrecked their cart.

# Type C: From *Julius Caesar*

<u>Essay Four Parallelism Edits</u>

**Phrase or Clause**
conspirators acted in secret

**Additional phrases or clauses**
Brutus served with fidelity
Caesar grew in popularity


**Phrase or Clause**
possibility of rejection

**Additional phrases or clauses**
of conflict
of dismissal

**Parallel structures**

Brutus should not have stabbed Caesar for three reasons: **Brutus served with fidelity, Caesar grew in popularity**, and the **conspirators acted in secret**.


Such secrecy avoided the possibility **of conflict, of rejection**, and **of dismissal** from opposing senators.

# ***ESSAY FIVE ELOCUTION: ANTITHESIS***

From Grimms' Tales for Young and Old, translated by Ralph Manheim

Their **faces** were **beautiful** and **lily-white**, but their **hearts** were **ugly** and **black**.

From Grahame's The Wind in the Willows

"I don't **talk about** my **river**," replied the patient Rat. "You know I don't, Toad. But I **think about it**," he added pathetically, in a lower tone: "I think about it—all the time!"

From Shakespeare's Julius Caesar

Act 1, Scene 2
The fault, dear Brutus, is not **in our stars,** but **in ourselves**, that we are underlings.

Act 2, Scene 1
Let us be **sacrificers**, but not **butchers**, Caius.

Let us kill him **boldly**, but not **wrathfully**;

Let's **carve him as a dish fit for the gods**, not **hew him as a carcass fit for hounds**:

Act 2, Scene 2
Dwell I but in the suburbs of your good pleasure? If it be no more, Portia is **Brutus' harlot**, not **his wife**.

Act 3, Scene 2
Not that **I loved Caesar less**, but that **I loved Rome more**.

Had you rather **Caesar were living**, and **die all slaves**, than that **Caesar were dead**, to **live all free men**?

I come **to bury Caesar**, not **to praise him**.

# Type A: From "Cinderella"

## Essay Five Antithesis Edits

**Idea to emphasize**
abuse

**Contrasting ideas**
serve, help, care

**Parallel structures**

Her stepmother and stepsisters **abused her**, but she **served them** without complaint.

**Idea to emphasize**
married a young man

**Contrasting ideas**
Cinderella hoped to dance
Prince desired to marry

**Cinderella hoped to dance** at the celebration, but the **prince desired to marry** a young maid.

# Type B: From *The Wind in the Willows*

## Essay Five Antithesis Edits

**Idea to emphasize**
hated spring cleaning

**Contrasting ideas**
loved fresh air
hated a dirty home

**Parallel structures**

He **hated a dirty home**, but **loved fresh air**.

**Idea to emphasize**
fell into trouble

**Contrasting ideas**
lift out of a snare

Mole learned how to make new friends whom he cared about and whom he could **lift out of a snare** when they **fell into trouble**.

# Type C: From *Julius Caesar*

## Essay Five Antithesis Edits

| | |
|---|---|
| **Idea to emphasize**<br>betray friends<br><br>**Contrasting ideas**<br>publicly celebrate life<br>secretly plot death | **Parallel structures**<br><br>What kind of man **publicly celebrates** his friend's **life**, but **secretly plots** his **death**? |
| **Idea to emphasize**<br>Caesar trusted Brutus with his life<br><br>**Contrasting ideas**<br>paid with his death | Caesar **trusted** Brutus **with his life**, but **paid with his death**. |
| **Idea to emphasize**<br>denied the crown<br><br>**Contrasting ideas**<br>offered an empire | The **people offered an empire**, but **Caesar denied the crown**. |

# **ESSAY SIX ELOCUTION: SIMILE**

From *Grimms' Tales for Young and Old*, translated by Ralph Manheim

She climbed among the branches **as nimbly as a squirrel** and the king's son didn't know what had become of her.


From Grahame's *The Wind in the Willows*

Glancing back, they saw a small cloud of dust, with a dark centre of energy, advancing on them at incredible speed, while from out the dust a faint "Poop-poop!" wailed **like an uneasy animal in pain**.

Breathless and transfixed the Mole stopped rowing as the liquid run of that glad piping broke on him **like a wave**, caught him up, and possessed him utterly.

The voice died away and ceased, **as an insect's tiny trumpet** dwindles swiftly into silence;


From Shakespeare's *Julius Caesar*

Act 1, Scene 1
I, **as Aeneas**, our great ancestor, did from the flames of Troy upon his shoulder the old Anchises bear, so from the waves of Tiber did I the tired Caesar.

I did hear him groan; Ay, and that tongue of his that bade the Romans mark him and write his speeches in their books, alas! it cried, 'Give me some drink, Titinius,' **as a sick girl**.

Act 1, Scene 3
A common slave—you know him well by sight—held up his left hand, which did flame and burn like twenty torches join'd; and yet his hand, not sensible of fire, remain'd unscorch'd.

Act 2, Scene 1
Let's carve him **as a dish** fit for the gods, not hew him as a carcass fit for hounds:

Act 3, Scene 1
But I am constant **as the northern star**, of whose true-fix'd and resting quality there is no fellow in the firmament.

Act 4, Scene 2
But hollow men, **like horses** hot at hand, make gallant show and promise of their mettle;

# Type A: From "Cinderella"

Essay Six Simile Edits

**Term**
change

**Characteristic or quality (list 4-5)**
turn, alter, adjust, move, sudden

**Thing of a different kind that shares one characteristic or quality**
winding river

**Simile**

**"is like"**
After Cinderella cleaned all the lentils with the help of the birds, her stepmother changed her mind like a winding river.

**"is as ADJECTIVE as . . ."**
After Cinderella cleaned all the lentils with the help of the birds, her stepmother changed her mind as suddenly as a winding river.

**Term**
Cinderella

**Characteristic or quality (list 4-5)**
beautiful, kind, humble, quiet

**Thing of a different kind that shares one characteristic or quality**
starry night

**Simile**

**"is like"**
Cinderella is like a starry night.

**"is as ADJECTIVE as . . ."**
Cinderella is as beautiful as a starry night.

# Type B: From *The Wind in the Willows*

<u>Essay Six Simile Edits</u>

**Term**
spring

**Characteristic or quality (list 4-5)**
fresh, new, exciting, living

**Thing of a different kind that shares one characteristic or quality**
a newborn child

**Simile**

**"is like"**
Spring is like a newborn child.

**"is as ADJECTIVE as . . ."**
Spring is as exciting as a newborn child.


**Term**
ran

**Characteristic or quality (list 4-5)**
push, shove, drive, force

**Thing of a different kind that shares one characteristic or quality**
a strong wind

**Simile**

**"is like"**
After lunch, Toad persuaded Mole to go on a road trip where an automobile like a strong wind ran them off the road, into a ditch, and wrecked their cart.

**"is as ADJECTIVE as . . ."**
After lunch, Toad persuaded Mole to go on a road trip where an automobile as forceful as a strong wind ran them off the road, into a ditch, and wrecked their cart.

# Type C: From *Julius Caesar*

Essay Six Simile Edits

**Term**
friend

**Characteristic or quality (list 4-5)**
loyal, trust, reliable, helps, true

**Thing of a different kind that shares one characteristic or quality**
sunrise

**Simile**

**"is like"**
A good friend is like a sunrise.

**"is as ADJECTIVE as . . ."**
A good friend is as reliable as the sunrise.


**Term**
Caesar

**Characteristic or quality (list 4-5)**
ambitious, proud, sly, powerful

**Thing of a different kind that shares one characteristic or quality**
fox

**Simile**

**"is like"**
Caesar is like a fox.

**"is as ADJECTIVE as . . ."**
Caesar is as sly as a fox.

# ESSAY SEVEN ELOCUTION: ALLITERATION

From *Grimms' Tales for Young and Old,* translated by Ralph Manheim

And they took to calling her Ashputtle because she always looked **dusty** and **dirty.**

Two little white doves came flying through the kitchen window, and then came the turtledoves, and finally all the birds under heaven came **flapping** and **fluttering** and settled down by the ashes.

Whereupon the bird tossed down a gold and silver dress and slippers embroidered with **silk** and **silver.**

From Grahame's *The Wind in the Willows*

Never in his life had he seen a river before—this **sleek, sinuous**, full-bodied animal, **chasing** and **chuckling, gripping** things with a **gurgle** and **leaving** them with a **laugh**, to **fling** itself on **fresh** playmates that shook themselves **free**, and were caught and held again.

Fastening their boat to a willow, the friends landed in this **silent, silver** kingdom, and patiently explored the **hedges**, the **hollow** trees, the tunnels and their little culverts, the **ditches** and **dry** waterways.

There he had a thorough wash and brush-up, changed his clothes, and stood for a long time before the glass, contemplating himself with **pride** and **pleasure**, and thinking what utter idiots all the people must have been to have ever mistaken him for one moment for a washerwoman.

From Shakespeare's *Julius Caesar*

Act 2, Scene 1
Swear priests and **cowards** and men **cautelous**, old feeble **carrions** and **such suffering souls** that **welcome wrongs**;

Act 3, Scene 2
And, in his **mantle muffling** up his face, even at the base of Pompey's status, which all the while ran blood, great Caesar fell.

For I have neither **wit**, nor **words**, nor **worth**, action, nor utterance, nor the power of speech, to stir men's blood:

Act 4, Scene 3
What! shall one of us, that struck the foremost man of all this world but for supporting robbers, shall we now contaminate our fingers with **base bribes**, and sell the mighty space of our large honours for so much trash as may be grasped thus?

# Type A: From "Cinderella"

## Essay Seven Alliteration Edits

**Seed-word**
"promised" from: After she asked, her stepmother promised that Cinderella could attend the celebration if she picked all the lentils out of the ashes within an hour.

**Consonant sound**
P

**Additional words with same consonant sound**
persuasively, passively, purposefully, playfully, posited, permit

**New sentence**
After she asked, her stepmother promised to permit that Cinderella could attend the celebration if she picked all the lentils out of the ashes within an hour.

**Seed-word**
"mocked" from: They mocked Cinderella and mistreated her.

**Consonant sound**
M

**Additional words with same consonant sound**
malicious, mean, miserable, maul, manage, meek

**New sentence**
They mocked the meek Cinderella and maliciously mistreated her.

# Type B: From *The Wind in the Willows*

Essay Seven Alliteration Edits

**Seed-word**
"calling" from: As he cleaned, he felt something calling him to leave what he was doing and climb up out of his hole.

**Consonant sound**
C

**Additional words with same consonant sound**
calmly, clearly, coolly, carelessly

**New sentence**
As he cleaned, he felt something carelessly calling him to leave what he was doing and climb up out of his hole.

**Seed-word**
"lived" from: At home, Mole lived alone.

**Consonant sound**
L

**Additional words with same consonant sound**
laughed, lounged, learned, laid, listened, looked, lulled

**New sentence**
At home, Mole lounged, lulled, and lived alone.

# Type C: From *Julius Caesar*

<u>Essay Seven Alliteration Edits</u>

**Seed-word**
"counsel" from: Though at first not favorable to the plan, Brutus is eventually won over by Cassius' persistent counsel.

**Consonant sound**
C

**Additional words with same consonant sound**
constant, clever, continuous, careful

**New sentence**
Though at first not favorable to the plan, Brutus is eventually won over by Cassius' clever counsel.

**Seed-word**
"rage" from: The fanned rage of the Roman citizens sparked by Caesar's death will turn upon the murderous ban of guilty senators.

**Consonant sound**
R

**Additional words with same consonant sound**
rising, roaring, riotous, rolling

**New sentence**
The riotous rage of the Roman citizens sparked by Caesar's death will turn upon the murderous ban of guilty senators.

# **_ESSAY EIGHT ELOCUTION: METAPHOR_**

<u>From Grimms' Tales for Young and Old, translated by Ralph Manheim</u>

When winter came, the snow spread a **white cloth** over the grave, and when spring took it off, the man remarried.


<u>From Grahame's The Wind in the Willows</u>

"And you really live by the river? What a jolly life!"

"By it and with it and on it and in it," said the Rat. "It's **brother** and **sister** to me, and **aunts**, and **company**, and **food** and **drink**, and (naturally) **washing**."

After a time he muttered gloomily, "I see it all now! What a **pig** I have been! A **pig**—that's me! Just a **pig**—a plain **pig**!"

The "poop-poop" rang with a brazen shout in their ears, they had a moment's glimpse of an interior of glittering plate-glass and rich morocco, and the magnificent motor-car, immense, breath-snatching, passionate, with its pilot tense and hugging his wheel, possessed all earth and air for the fraction of a second, flung an enveloping cloud of dust that blinded and en-wrapped them utterly, and then dwindled to a speck in the far distance, changed back into a **droning bee** once more.


<u>From Shakespeare's Julius Caesar</u>

Act 1, Scene 1
You **blocks**, you **stones**, you worse than **senseless things**!

These growing **feathers** pluck'd from **Caesar's wing** will make him **fly** an ordinary pitch, who else would **soar** above the view of men and keep us all in servile fearfulness.

And **this man is now become a god**, and Cassius is a wretched creature and must bend his body if Caesar carelessly but nod on him.

Act 1, Scene 3
And why should Caesar be a tyrant then? Poor man! I know he would not be a **wolf** but that he sees the **Romans are but sheep**; He were no **lion** were not **Romans hinds**.

Act 2, Scene 2
**We are two lions** litter'd in one day, and I the elder and more terrible: And Caesar shall go forth.

Act 3, Scene 2
I tell you that which you yourselves do know, show you **sweet Caesar's wounds, poor poor dumb mouths**, and bid them **speak** for me:

# Type A: From "Cinderella"

Essay Eight Metaphor Edits

**Term**
father

**Trait or action**
neglectful, abandons Cinderella

**Thing of a different kind that manifests the same trait or action**
stag

**Metaphor**
Cinderella's father is a stag, abandoning his offspring to the care of the herd.

**Term**
stepmother

**Trait or action**
toying with Cinderella

**Thing of a different kind that manifests the same trait or action**
cat

**Metaphor**
Her stepmother was a cat toying with Cinderella by keeping her home for no just reason.

# Type B: From *The Wind in the Willows*

Essay Eight Metaphor Edits

**Term**
friend

**Trait or action**
supportive

**Thing of a different kind that manifests the same trait or action**
bulwark

**Metaphor**
Good friends are a supportive bulwark that protects against many dangers.

**Term**
impatience

**Trait or action**
drives, pushes, impels

**Thing of a different kind that manifests the same trait or action**
favorable wind

**Metaphor**
A favorable wind is driving Mole to leave his home for fresh air and a change.

# Type C: From *Julius Caesar*

## Essay Eight Metaphor Edits

**Term**
Roman people

**Trait or action**
gather around leader

**Thing of a different kind that manifests the same trait or action**
a flock

**Metaphor**
Caesar returned to his flock in Rome as a hero.

**Term**
senators

**Trait or action**
surprised, startled

**Thing of a different kind that manifests the same trait or action**
squirrel

**Metaphor**
Many of the senators were startled squirrels knowing nothing of the plot and played no part in carrying out this murderous act.

# ***ESSAY NINE ELOCUTION: ASSONANCE***

From *Grimms' Tales for Young and Old,* translated by Ralph Manheim

"O tame little doves, O turtledoves, and all the birds under heaven, come and help me put the good ones in the **pot,**
the bad ones in your **crop**."


From Grahame's *The Wind in the Willows*

"Up we go! Up we go!" till at last, pop! his **snout** came **out** into the sunlight, and he found himself rolling in the warm grass of a great meadow.

I came up this backwater to try and get a moment's **peace**, and then stumble upon you fellows!—At **least**—I beg pardon—I don't exactly **mean** that, you know."

On the sands they had horses waiting, which dragged the casks upon the **steep street** of the little town with a fine rush and clatter and scramble.

Those eyes were of the changing foam-**streaked** grey-green of **leaping** Northern **seas**; in the glass shone a hot ruby that **seemed** the very heart of the South, **beating** for him who had courage to respond to its pulsation.


From Shakespeare's *Julius Caesar*

Act 1, Scene 1
What **trade**, thou **knave**? thou naughty **knave**, what **trade**?

Act 1, Scene 2
Men at some time are masters of their fates: the fault, dear Brutus, is not in **our stars**, but in **ourselves**, that we **are** underlings.

Act 3, Scene 2
O judgment! thou art fled to brutish **beasts**, and men have lost their **reason**.

Act 4, Scene 1
But **hollow** men, like **horses hot** at hand, make gallant **show** and promise of their mettle; but when they should **endure** the bloody **spur**, they fall their crests, and like deceitful jades, sink in the trial.

Act 4, Scene 3
What! shall one of us, that struck the **foremost** man of all this **world** but for **supporting** robbers, shall we now contaminate our fingers with base bribes, and sell the mighty space of our large honours for so much **trash** as may be **grasped** thus?

# Type A: From "Cinderella"

<u>Essay Nine Assonance Edits</u>

**Seed-word**
meet

**Vowel sound**
EE

**Additional words with same vowel sound**
feet, seek, leak, speak, feat, great, beat, treat, neat, free

**New sentence**
She could meet the prince, seek her freedom, and leave her home.


**Seed-word**
served

**Vowel sound**
short E

**Additional words with same vowel sound**
her, tortured, bird, earned, worship, further

**New sentence**
Her new family tortured her, but she served them without further complaint.

# Type B: From *The Wind in the Willows*

<u>Essay Nine Assonance Edits</u>

**Seed-word**
lived

**Vowel sound**
short I

**Additional words with same vowel sound**
river, dinner, in, shiver, spin, swim, hither, thither, visited

**New sentence**
The first new friend Mole visited, Ratty, lived on and in and near the river.


**Seed-word**
trouble

**Vowel sound**
OU

**Additional words with same vowel sound**
bubble, stub, up, snug, rough, shove, fumble

**New sentence**
By leaving home, Mole learned how to make new friends whom he cared about and whom he could lift up out of a rough spot when they stumbled into trouble.

# Type C: From *Julius Caesar*

<u>Essay Nine Assonance Edits</u>

**Seed-word**
leader

**Vowel sound**
EA

**Additional words with same vowel sound**
Caesar, beat, feet, meet, fear, dear

**New sentence**
Every Roman agrees that Caesar is an important and fearless leader.


**Seed-word**
led

**Vowel sound**
short E

**Additional words with same vowel sound**
sped, dead, shed, said, head, fed, read, steady

**New sentence**
The ambitious head led his steady army into the city, which not only threatened a free Rome, but sped towards the first steps of tyranny.

Part Four
# Essays

# ***ESSAY ONE: RUDIMENTARY PERSUASIVE ESSAY***

I. Introduction
    A. Thesis
    B. Enumeration
    C. Exposition
        1.
        2.
        3.

II. Proof
    A.
    B.
    C.

III. Conclusion
    A. Thesis
    B. Summary of Proof
        1.
        2.
        3.

## Type A: From "Cinderella"

Cinderella should have gone to the celebration for three reasons: The king invited all the beautiful girls in the kingdom, her stepmother promised she could go, and she does not have a husband.

The first reason Cinderella should have gone to the celebration is that the king invited all the beautiful girls in the kingdom. The second reason Cinderella should have gone to the celebration is that her stepmother promised she could go. The third reason Cinderella should have gone to the celebration is that she does not have a husband.

Cinderella should have gone to the celebration because the king invited all the beautiful girls in the kingdom, her stepmother promised she could go, and she does not have a husband.

# Type B: From *The Wind in the Willows*

Mole should have left his home for three reasons: He was alone, he did not like spring cleaning, and he met new friends.

The first reason Mole should have left his home is that he was alone. The second reason Mole should have left his home is that he did not like spring cleaning. The third reason Mole should have left his home is that he met new friends.

Mole should have left his home because he was alone, he did not like spring cleaning, and he met new friends.

# Type C: From *Julius Caesar*

Brutus should not have stabbed Caesar for three reasons: Caesar trusted Brutus, the people supported Caesar, and Brutus was a respected leader of Rome.

The first reason Brutus should not have stabbed Caesar is that Caesar trusted Brutus. The second reason Brutus should not have stabbed Caesar is that the people supported Caesar. The third reason Brutus should not have stabbed Caesar is that Brutus was a respected leader of Rome.

Brutus should not have stabbed Caesar because Caesar trusted Brutus, the people supported Caesar, and Brutus was a respected leader of Rome.

# ***ESSAY TWO: INTRODUCTORY PERSUASIVE ESSAY***

I. Introduction
    A. Thesis
    B. Enumeration
    C. Exposition
        1.
        2.
        3.

II. Proof
    A. Proof 1
        **1. support for proof 1**
        **2. support for proof 1**
        **3. support for proof 1**
    B. Proof 2
        **1. support for proof 2**
        **2. support for proof 2**
        **3. support for proof 2**
    C. Proof 3
        **1. support for proof 3**
        **2. support for proof 3**
        **3. support for proof 3**

III. Conclusion
    A. Thesis
    B. Summary of Proof
        1.
        2.
        3.

## Type A: From "Cinderella"

Cinderella should have gone to the celebration for three reasons: marriage, she had permission, and her family did not love her.

The first reason Cinderella should have gone to the celebration is marriage. **The king had invited all the beautiful girls in the kingdom to the palace for a three-day marriage celebration for his son. Cinderella did not yet have a husband. She could possibly meet the prince and become his bride.**

The second reason Cinderella should have gone to the celebration is that she had permission. **After she asked, her stepmother said Cinderella could go to the celebration if she picked all the lentils out of the ashes within an hour. After Cinderella got all the lentils with the help of the birds, her stepmother changed her mind. However, Cinderella was helped again by a bird in the hazel tree who gave Cinderella a dress for the celebration.**

The third reason Cinderella should have gone to the celebration is that her family did not love her. **Cinderella lived with her *father, stepmother, and stepsisters*. Her stepmother and stepsisters were cruel. They made fun of Cinderella and mistreated her. Cinderella was also not loved by her father.**

Cinderella should have gone to the celebration because of marriage, she had permission, and her family did not love her.

# Type B: From *The Wind in the Willows*

Mole should have left his *safe, comfortable, and peaceful* home for three reasons: It was a new spring, he could meet new friends, and he could go on new adventures.

The first reason Mole should have left his *safe, comfortable, and peaceful* home is that it was a new spring. **While he was cleaning the house, Mole could sense something calling him. He did not like spring cleaning and wanted to go up out of his home to enjoy the spring. Once out of his hole, he could experience the world above ground.**

The second reason Mole should have left his *safe, comfortable, and peaceful* home is that he could meet new friends. **At home, Mole was alone. The first new friend Mole met was Ratty who lived on the river. Afterwards, Mole met Badger, who lived in the Wild Wood.**

The third reason Mole should have left his *safe, comfortable, and peaceful* home is that he could go on new adventures. **Mole had never seen any home as nice as Toad Hall, where he ate lunch with Toad and Ratty. After lunch, he was persuaded by Toad to go on a road trip, where an automobile ran them off the road and wrecked their cart. Mole also helped Toad save his home from the Weasels, who took Toad Hall while Toad was in jail.**

Mole should have left his *safe, comfortable, and peaceful* home because it was a new spring, he could meet new friends, and he could go on new adventures.

## Type C: From *Julius Caesar*

Brutus should not have stabbed Caesar for three reasons: *Brutus* is trustworthy, *Caesar* earned the people's favor, and the *Senate* is not united.

The first reason Brutus should not have stabbed Caesar is that Brutus is trustworthy. **Caesar trusted Brutus with his life believing that with a friend such as Brutus there would never be an attempt to kill him. Not only was Brutus trusted by Caesar, but the Roman people also looked to Brutus as a respected and trustworthy leader of Rome.**

The second reason Brutus should not have stabbed Caesar is that Caesar earned the people's favor. **Caesar returned to Rome as a hero in the eyes of the Roman people. The Romans loved and supported Caesar. In fact, they loved him so much that they wanted to make him emperor by offering him the crown. Yet, Caesar denied the crown three times for everyone to see.**

The third reason Brutus should not have stabbed Caesar is that the Senate is not united. **It is important to note that only some of the senators joined the plot to assassinate Caesar. Many of the senators were unaware of the plot and played no part in carrying out this murderous act. Such secrecy kept a vote off of the Senate floor.**

Brutus should not have stabbed Caesar because *Brutus* is trustworthy, *Caesar* earned the people's favor, and the *Senate* is not united.

# ESSAY THREE: BASIC PERSUASIVE ESSAY I

I. Introduction
    **A. Exordium**
    B. Thesis
    C. Enumeration
    D. Exposition
        1.
        2.
        3.

II. Proof
    A. Proof 1
        1.
        2.
        3.
    B. Proof 2
        1.
        2.
        3.
    C. Proof 3
        1.
        2.
        3.

III. Conclusion
    A. Thesis
    B. Summary of Proof
        1.
        2.
        3.

Type A: From *"Cinderella"*

**Seize opportunity while it lasts.** Cinderella should have gone to the celebration for three reasons: marriage, she *received* permission, and her family did not love her.

The first reason Cinderella should have gone to the celebration is marriage. The king had invited all the beautiful girls in the kingdom to the palace for a three-day marriage celebration for his son. Cinderella had not yet *married* a young man. She could possibly meet the prince and become his bride.

The second reason Cinderella should have gone to the celebration is that she *received* permission. After she asked, her stepmother *promised* that Cinderella could attend the celebration if she picked all the lentils out of the ashes within an hour. After Cinderella *cleaned* all the lentils with the help of the birds, her stepmother changed her mind. However, another bird *helped* Cinderella when it *tossed* down a dress out of the hazel tree for the celebration.

The third reason Cinderella should have gone to the celebration is that her family did not love her. Cinderella lived with her father, stepmother, and stepsisters. Her stepmother and stepsisters *abused* her. They *mocked* Cinderella and mistreated her. Also, Cinderella's father did not love her.

Cinderella should have gone to the celebration because of marriage, she *received* permission, and her family did not love her.

## Type B: From *The Wind in the Willows*

**"Something up above was calling him imperiously, and he made for the steep little tunnel."** Mole should have left his safe, comfortable, and peaceful home for three reasons: A new spring *had arrived*, he could meet new friends, and he could *experience* new adventures.

The first reason Mole should have left his safe, comfortable, and peaceful home is that a new spring *had arrived*. While he was cleaning the house, Mole could sense something calling him. He *hated* spring cleaning and wanted to climb up out of his home to enjoy the spring. Once out of his hole, he could *experience* the world above ground.

The second reason Mole should have left his safe, comfortable, and peaceful home is that he could meet new friends. At home, Mole *lived* alone. The first new friend Mole met, Ratty, lived on the river. Afterwards, Mole met Badger, who lived in the Wild Wood.

The third reason Mole should have left his safe, comfortable, and peaceful home is that he could *experience* new adventures. Mole had never seen any home as nice as Toad Hall, where he ate lunch with Toad and Ratty. After lunch, Toad *persuaded* Mole to go on a road trip where an automobile ran them off the road and wrecked their cart. Mole also helped Toad save his home from the Weasels who *invaded* Toad Hall while Toad *served* time in jail.

Mole should have left his safe, comfortable, and peaceful home because a new spring had *arrived*, he could meet new friends, and he could *experience* new adventures.

Type C: From *Julius Caesar*

**What kind of man betrays his friends?** Brutus should not have stabbed Caesar for three reasons: The people *trusted* Brutus, Caesar *earned* the people's favor, and the conspirators *acted* in secret.

The first reason Brutus should not have stabbed Caesar is that the people *trusted* Brutus. Caesar trusted Brutus with his life believing that with a friend such as Brutus there would never be an attempt to kill him. Not only did Caesar *trust* Brutus, but the Roman people also looked to Brutus as a respected and trustworthy leader of Rome.

The second reason Brutus should not have stabbed Caesar is that Caesar *earned* the people's favor. Caesar returned to Rome as a hero in the eyes of the Roman people. The Romans loved and supported Caesar. In fact, they loved him so much that they *desired* to crown Caesar emperor. Yet, Caesar denied the crown three times for everyone to see.

The third reason Brutus should not have stabbed Caesar is that the conspirators *acted* in secret. Only some of the senators joined the plot to assassinate Caesar. Many of the senators *knew* nothing of the plot and played no part in carrying out this murderous act. Such secrecy *avoided* the possibility of rejection from opposing senators.

Brutus should not have stabbed Caesar because the people *trusted* Brutus, Caesar *earned* the people's favor, and the conspirators *acted* in secret.

# *ESSAY FOUR: BASIC PERSUASIVE ESSAY II*

I. Introduction
    A. Exordium
    B. Thesis
    C. Enumeration
    D. Exposition
        1.
        2.
        3.

II. Proof
    A. Proof 1
        1.
        2.
        3.
    B. Proof 2
        1.
        2.
        3.
    C. Proof 3
        1.
        2.
        3.

III. Conclusion
    A. Thesis
    B. Summary of Proof
        1.
        2.
        3.
    **C. Amplification**
        **1. To whom it matters**
        **2. Why it matters**

# Type A: From *"Cinderella"*

Seize opportunity while it lasts. Cinderella should have gone to the celebration for three reasons: She *accepted the invitation, received permission,* and *suffered abandonment.*

The first reason Cinderella should have gone to the celebration is that she *accepted the invitation*. The king had invited all the beautiful girls in the kingdom to the palace for a three-day marriage celebration for his son. Cinderella had not yet married a young man. She could possibly *meet the prince, become his bride,* and *leave her home*.

The second reason Cinderella should have gone to the celebration is that she received permission. After she asked, her stepmother promised that Cinderella could attend the celebration if she picked all the lentils out of the ashes within an hour. After Cinderella cleaned all the lentils with the help of the birds, her stepmother changed her mind. However, another bird helped Cinderella when it tossed down a dress out of the hazel tree for the celebration.

The third reason Cinderella should have gone to the celebration is that she suffered abandonment. Cinderella lived with her father, stepmother, and stepsisters. Her stepmother and stepsisters abused her. They mocked Cinderella and mistreated her. Also, Cinderella's father did not love her.

Cinderella should have gone to the celebration because she *accepted the invitation, received permission,* and *suffered abandonment*. **By going to the celebration, Cinderella meets the prince who falls in love with her and wants to make her his wife.**

# Type B: From *The Wind in the Willows*

"Something up above was calling him imperiously, and he made for the steep little tunnel. . ." Mole should have left his safe, comfortable, and peaceful home for three reasons: He wanted to *enjoy the new spring*, *to meet new friends*, and *to experience new adventures*.

The first reason Mole should have left his safe, comfortable, and peaceful home is that he wanted to enjoy the new spring. While he was cleaning the house, Mole could sense something calling him. He hated spring cleaning and wanted to climb up out of his home to enjoy the spring. Once out of his hole, he could experience the world above ground.

The second reason Mole should have left his safe, comfortable, and peaceful home is that he wanted to meet new friends. At home, Mole lived alone. The first new friend Mole met, Ratty, lived on the river. Afterwards, Mole met Badger, who lived in the Wild Wood.

The third reason Mole should have left his safe, comfortable, and peaceful home is that he wanted to experience new adventures. Mole had never seen any home as nice as Toad Hall, where he ate lunch with Toad and Ratty. After lunch, Toad persuaded Mole to go on a road trip, where an automobile ran them *off the road*, *into a ditch*, and wrecked their cart. Mole also helped Toad save his home from the Weasels, who invaded Toad Hall while Toad served time in jail.

Mole should have left his safe, comfortable, and peaceful home because he wanted to *enjoy the new spring*, *to meet new friends*, and *to experience new adventures*. **By leaving home, Mole learned how to make new friends whom he cared about and was able to help when they fell into trouble.**

# Type C: From *Julius Caesar*

What kind of man betrays his friends? Brutus should not have stabbed Caesar for three reasons: *Brutus served with fidelity*, *Caesar grew in popularity*, and the *conspirators acted in secret*.

The first reason Brutus should not have stabbed Caesar is that Brutus served with fidelity. Caesar trusted Brutus with his life believing that with a friend such as Brutus there would never be an attempt to kill him. Not only did Caesar trust Brutus, but the Roman people also looked to Brutus as a respected and trustworthy leader of Rome.

The second reason Brutus should not have stabbed Caesar is that Caesar grew in popularity. Caesar returned to Rome as a hero in the eyes of the Roman people. The Romans loved and supported Caesar. In fact, they loved him so much that they desired to crown Caesar emperor. Yet, Caesar denied the crown three times for everyone to see.

The third reason Brutus should not have stabbed Caesar is that the conspirators acted in secret. Only some of the senators joined the plot to assassinate Caesar. Many of the senators knew nothing of the plot and played no part in carrying out this murderous act. Such secrecy avoided the possibility *of conflict*, *of rejection*, and *of dismissal* from opposing senators.

Brutus should not have stabbed Caesar because *Brutus served with fidelity*, *Caesar grew in popularity*, and the *conspirators acted in secret*. **The fanned rage of the Roman citizens sparked by Caesar's death will turn upon the murderous ban of guilty senators.**

# *ESSAY FIVE: BASIC PERSUASIVE ESSAY III*

I. Introduction
   A. Exordium
   **B. Division**
       **1. Agreement**
       **2. Disagreement**
          **a. Thesis**
          **b. Counter-Thesis**
   C. Distribution
       1. Thesis
       2. Enumeration
       3. Exposition
          a.
          b.
          c.

II. Proof
   A. Proof 1
       1.
       2.
       3.
   B. Proof 2
       1.
       2.
       3.
   C. Proof 3
       1.
       2.
       3.

III. Conclusion
   A. Thesis
   B. Summary of Proof
       1.
       2.
       3.
   C. Amplification
       1. To whom it matters
       2. Why it matters

# Type A: From *"Cinderella"*

Seize opportunity while it lasts. **Everyone agrees that Cinderella is invited to the celebration, but some believe that Cinderella should have gone to the celebration and some believe that she should not have gone to the celebration**. Cinderella should have gone to the celebration for three reasons: She accepted the invitation, received permission, and suffered abandonment.

The first reason Cinderella should have gone to the celebration is that she accepted the invitation. The king had invited all the beautiful girls in the kingdom to the palace for a three-day marriage celebration for his son. *Cinderella hoped to dance* at the celebration, *but the prince desired to marry* a young maid. She could possibly meet the prince, become his bride, and leave her home.

The second reason Cinderella should have gone to the celebration is that she received permission. After she asked, her stepmother promised that Cinderella could attend the celebration if she picked all the lentils out of the ashes within an hour. After Cinderella cleaned all the lentils with the help of the birds, her stepmother changed her mind. However, another bird helped Cinderella when it tossed down a dress out of the hazel tree for the celebration.

The third reason Cinderella should have gone to the celebration is that she suffered abandonment. Cinderella lived with her father, stepmother, and stepsisters. Her stepmother and stepsisters *abused her*, but she *served them* without complaint. They mocked Cinderella and mistreated her. Also, Cinderella's father did not love her.

Cinderella should have gone to the celebration because she accepted the invitation, received permission, and suffered abandonment. By going to the celebration, Cinderella meets the prince who falls in love with her and wants to make her his wife.

## Type B: From *The Wind in the Willows*

"Something up above was calling him imperiously, and he made for the steep little tunnel." **Everyone agrees that a home provides comfort and protection, but some believe that Mole should have left his home and some believe that he should not have left his home.** Mole should have left his safe, comfortable, and peaceful home for three reasons: He wanted to enjoy the new spring, to meet new friends, and to experience new adventures.

The first reason Mole should have left his safe, comfortable, and peaceful home is that he wanted to enjoy the new spring. While he was cleaning the house, Mole could sense something calling him. He *hated a dirty home*, but *loved fresh air*. Mole wanted to climb up out of his home to enjoy the spring. Once out of his hole, he could experience the world above ground.

The second reason Mole should have left his safe, comfortable, and peaceful home is that he wanted to meet new friends. At home, Mole lived alone. The first new friend Mole met, Ratty, lived on the river. Afterwards, Mole met Badger, who lived in the Wild Wood.

The third reason Mole should have left his safe, comfortable, and peaceful home is that he wanted to experience new adventures. Mole had never seen any home as nice as Toad Hall, where he ate lunch with Toad and Ratty. After lunch, Toad persuaded Mole to go on a road trip, where an automobile ran them off the road, into a ditch, and wrecked their cart. Mole also helped Toad save his home from the Weasels, who invaded Toad Hall while Toad served time in jail.

Mole should have left his safe, comfortable, and peaceful home because he wanted to enjoy the new spring, to meet new friends, and to experience new adventures. By leaving home, Mole learned how to make new friends whom he cared about and whom he could *lift out of a snare* when they *fell into trouble*.

## Type C: From *Julius Caesar*

What kind of man *publicly celebrates his friend's life*, but *secretly plots his death*? **Every Roman agrees that Caesar is an important leader, but some believe that Brutus should not have stabbed Caesar and some believe that he should have stabbed Caesar.** Brutus should not have stabbed Caesar for three reasons: Brutus served with fidelity, Caesar grew in popularity, and the conspirators acted in secret.

The first reason Brutus should not have stabbed Caesar is that Brutus served with fidelity. Caesar trusted Brutus with his life believing that with a friend such as Brutus there would never be an attempt to kill him. Not only did Caesar trust Brutus, but the Roman people also looked to Brutus as a respected and trustworthy leader of Rome.

The second reason Brutus should not have stabbed Caesar is that Caesar grew in popularity. Caesar returned to Rome as a hero in the eyes of the Roman people. The Romans loved and supported Caesar. In fact, they loved him so much that they desired to crown Caesar emperor. Yet, Caesar denied the crown three times for everyone to see.

The third reason Brutus should not have stabbed Caesar is that the conspirators acted in secret. Only some of the senators joined the plot to assassinate Caesar. Many of the senators knew nothing of the plot and played no part in carrying out this murderous act. Such secrecy avoided the possibility of conflict, of rejection, and of dismissal from opposing senators.

Brutus should not have stabbed Caesar because Brutus served with fidelity, Caesar grew in popularity, and the conspirators acted in secret. The fanned rage of the Roman citizens sparked by Caesar's death will turn upon the murderous ban of guilty senators.

# ESSAY SIX: BASIC PERSUASIVE ESSAY IV

I. Introduction
    A. Exordium
    B. Division
        1. Agreement
        2. Disagreement
            a. Thesis
            b. Counter-Thesis
    C. Distribution
        1. Thesis
        2. Enumeration
        3. Exposition
            a.
            b.
            c.

II. Proof
    A. Proof 1
        1.
        2.
        3.
    B. Proof 2
        1.
        2.
        3.
    C. Proof 3
        1.
        2.
        3.

**III. Refutation**
    **A. Counter-Thesis**
    **B. Counter-Proof 1**
        **1. Summary of support for reason 1**
        **2. Inadequacy of reason 1**
    **C. Counter-Proof 2**
        **1. Summary of support for reason 2**
        **2. Inadequacy of reason 2**
    **D. Summary of Refutation**

IV. Conclusion
    A. Thesis
    B. Summary of Proof
        1.
        2.
        3.
    C. Amplification
        1. To whom it matters
        2. Why it matters

# Type A: From *"Cinderella"*

Seize opportunity while it lasts. Everyone agrees that Cinderella is invited to the celebration, but some believe that Cinderella should have gone to the celebration and some believe that she should not have gone to the celebration. Cinderella should have gone to the celebration for three reasons: She accepted the invitation, received permission, and suffered abandonment.

The first reason Cinderella should have gone to the celebration is that she accepted the invitation. Cinderella is *as beautiful as a starry night*. The king had invited all the beautiful girls in the kingdom to the palace for a three-day marriage celebration for his son. Cinderella hoped to dance at the celebration, but the prince desired to marry a young maid. She could possibly meet the prince, become his bride, and leave her home.

The second reason Cinderella should have gone to the celebration is that she received permission. After she asked, her stepmother promised that Cinderella could attend the celebration if she picked all the lentils out of the ashes within an hour. After Cinderella cleaned all the lentils with the help of the birds, her stepmother changed her mind *as suddenly as a winding river*. However, another bird helped Cinderella when it tossed down a dress out of the hazel tree for the celebration.

The third reason Cinderella should have gone to the celebration is that she suffered abandonment. Cinderella lived with her father, stepmother, and stepsisters. Her stepmother and stepsisters abused her, but she served them without complaint. They mocked Cinderella and mistreated her. Also, Cinderella's father did not love her.

**Some argue that Cinderella should not have gone to the celebration. She needs to follow instructions. Her stepmother told her to stay home, and her real mother instructed her to be good. Cinderella must obey her parents. However, Cinderella was unfairly prohibited from attending the celebration by her stepmother, who despised her. Her stepmother had no just reason for keeping Cinderella at home.**

**Others argue that Cinderella was not ready to go to the celebration. She did not have a dress and she did not know how to dance. Also, Cinderella did not clean the lentils herself. The birds helped her by cleaning all of the lentils. Even though Cinderella was not ready to attend the celebration, she received help from the birds who lived in the tree at her mother's grave. After receiving their help, Cinderella was ready to attend the celebration.**

**Neither the need to follow instructions nor Cinderella's unpreparedness for attending the celebration provides sufficient reason for prohibiting Cinderella from going to the celebration.**

Cinderella should have gone to the celebration because she accepted the invitation, received permission, and suffered abandonment. By going to the celebration, Cinderella meets the prince who falls in love with her and wants to make her his wife.

# Type B: From *The Wind in the Willows*

"Something up above was calling him imperiously, and he made for the steep little tunnel." Everyone agrees that a home provides comfort and protection, but some believe that Mole should have left his home and some believe that he should not have left his home. Mole should have left his safe, comfortable, and peaceful home for three reasons: He wanted to enjoy the new spring, to meet new friends, and to experience new adventures.

The first reason Mole should have left his safe, comfortable, and peaceful home is that he wanted to enjoy the new spring. While he was cleaning the house, Mole could sense something calling him. He hated a dirty home, but loved fresh air. *Spring is like a newborn child*. Mole wanted to climb up out of his home to enjoy the spring. Once out of his hole, he could experience the world above ground.

The second reason Mole should have left his safe, comfortable, and peaceful home is that he wanted to meet new friends. At home, Mole lived alone. The first new friend Mole met, Ratty, lived on the river. Afterwards, Mole met Badger, who lived in the Wild Wood.

The third reason Mole should have left his safe, comfortable, and peaceful home is that he wanted to experience new adventures. Mole had never seen any home as nice as Toad Hall, where he ate lunch with Toad and Ratty. After lunch, Toad persuaded Mole to go on a road trip, where an automobile *like a strong wind* ran them off the road, into a ditch, and wrecked their cart. Mole also helped Toad save his home from the Weasels, who invaded Toad Hall while Toad served time in jail.

**Some argue that Mole should not have left his home. The world above ground contained too many dangers. After leaving home, Mole fell out of Ratty's boat into the river. Later, he wandered into the Wild Wood, losing his way. Mole also risked losing his home to someone else who might have taken it. The possibility of danger does not make danger certain. Because something might happen does not mean that it will happen.**

**Others argue that Mole lacked patience. He threw down his brush before he finished cleaning his home. Mole lived safely and comfortably in his home free from any danger. The spring air distracted Mole from the security of his home. However, Mole's impatience is not a reason to stay home. It actually gives him more reason to leave his home for fresh air and a change.**

**Neither the possibility of danger nor Mole's impatience provides sufficient reason for Mole to have stayed home.**

Mole should have left his safe, comfortable, and peaceful home because he wanted to enjoy the new spring, to meet new friends, and to experience new adventures. By leaving home, Mole learned how to make new friends whom he cared about and whom he could lift out of a snare when they fell into trouble.

# Type C: From *Julius Caesar*

What kind of man publicly celebrates his friend's life, but secretly plots his death? Every Roman agrees that Caesar is an important leader, but some believe that Brutus should not have stabbed Caesar and some believe that he should have stabbed Caesar. Brutus should not have stabbed Caesar for three reasons: Brutus served with fidelity, Caesar grew in popularity, and the conspirators acted in secret.

The first reason Brutus should not have stabbed Caesar is that Brutus served with fidelity. A good friend is *as reliable as the sunrise*. Caesar trusted Brutus with his life believing that with a friend such as Brutus there would never be an attempt to kill him. Not only did Caesar trust Brutus, but the Roman people also looked to Brutus as a respected and trustworthy leader of Rome.

The second reason Brutus should not have stabbed Caesar is that Caesar grew in popularity. Caesar returned to Rome as a hero in the eyes of the Roman people. The Romans loved and supported Caesar. In fact, they loved him so much that they desired to crown Caesar emperor. Yet, Caesar denied the crown three times for everyone to see.

The third reason Brutus should not have stabbed Caesar is that the conspirators acted in secret. Only some of the senators joined the plot to assassinate Caesar. Many of the senators knew nothing of the plot and played no part in carrying out this murderous act. Such secrecy avoided the possibility of conflict, of rejection, and of dismissal from opposing senators.

**Some have argued that Brutus should have stabbed Caesar. Caesar was *as sly as a fox*. The ambitious leader led his army into the city, which not only threatened a free Rome, but marked the first steps toward tyranny. However, Caesar's lust for power required political action, not military. Brutus, not Caesar, turned the Senate floor into a battlefield.**

**Others argued that Brutus' love for Rome was greater than his love for Caesar. Caesar loved Rome no less than Brutus. The notion that Caesar threatened the liberty of Rome lacked sufficient evidence and emerged more from the irrational fears of a few men than the temperate love of the multitude.**

**Neither the argument that Caesar intended to use his military strength to enslave Rome nor the argument that Brutus acted out of a greater love than Caesar for the good of Rome provides sufficient reason for assassinating a man loved by those whom he served to protect.**

Brutus should not have stabbed Caesar because Brutus served with fidelity, Caesar grew in popularity, and the conspirators acted in secret. The fanned rage of the Roman citizens sparked by Caesar's death will turn upon the murderous ban of guilty senators.

# **ESSAY SEVEN: COMPLETE PERSUASIVE ESSAY**

I. Introduction
    A. Exordium
    **B. Narratio**
        **1. Situation**
        **2. Actions**
    C. Division
        1. Agreement
        2. Disagreement
            a. Thesis
            b. Counter-Thesis
    D. Distribution
        1. Thesis
        2. Enumeration
        3. Exposition
            a.
            b.
            c.

II. Proof
    A. Proof 1
        1.
        2.
        3.
    B. Proof 2
        1.
        2.
        3.
    C. Proof 3
        1.
        2.
        3.

III. Refutation
    A. Counter-Thesis
    B. Counter-Proof 1
        1. Summary of support for reason 1
        2. Inadequacy of reason 1
    C. Counter-Proof 2
        1. Summary of support for reason 2
        2. Inadequacy of reason 2
    D. Summary of Refutation

IV. Conclusion
    A. Thesis
    B. Summary of Proof
        1.
        2.
        3.
    C. Amplification
        1. To whom it matters
        2. Why it matters

## Type A: From *"Cinderella"*

Seize opportunity while it lasts. **One spring the king wanted to find a wife for his son so he invited all of the beautiful girls in the kingdom to attend a three-day celebration. Cinderella asked her stepmother if she could go, but her stepmother told her that she was dirty, did not have a dress, and could not dance. After she begged to go, the stepmother dumped a bowl of lentils in a pile of ashes and said that she could go if all the lentils were cleaned in one hour. When Cinderella finished the task, her stepmother repeated that Cinderella could not go to the celebration.**

Everyone agrees that Cinderella is invited to the celebration, but some believe that Cinderella should have gone to the celebration and some believe that she should not have gone to the celebration. Cinderella should have gone to the celebration for three reasons: She accepted the invitation, received permission, and suffered abandonment.

The first reason Cinderella should have gone to the celebration is that she accepted the invitation. Cinderella is as beautiful as a starry night. The king had invited all the beautiful girls in the kingdom to the palace for a three-day marriage celebration for his son. Cinderella hoped to dance at the celebration, but the prince desired to marry a young maid. She could possibly meet the prince, become his bride, and leave her home.

The second reason Cinderella should have gone to the celebration is that she received permission. After she asked, her stepmother *promised to permit* that Cinderella could attend the celebration if she *picked* all the lentils out of the ashes within an hour. After Cinderella cleaned all the lentils with the help of the birds, her stepmother changed her mind as suddenly as a winding river. However, another bird helped Cinderella when it tossed down a dress out of the hazel tree for the celebration.

The third reason Cinderella should have gone to the celebration is that she suffered abandonment. Cinderella lived with her father, stepmother, and stepsisters. Her stepmother and stepsisters abused her, but she served them without complaint. They *mocked* the *meek* Cinderella and *maliciously mistreated* her. Also, Cinderella's father did not love her.

Some argue that Cinderella should not have gone to the celebration. She needs to follow instructions. Her stepmother told her to stay home, and her real mother instructed her to be good. Cinderella must obey her parents. However, Cinderella was unfairly prohibited from attending the celebration by her stepmother, who despised her. Her stepmother had no just reason for keeping Cinderella at home.

Others argue that Cinderella was not ready to go to the celebration. She did not have a dress and she did not know how to dance. Also, Cinderella did not clean the lentils herself. The birds helped her by cleaning all of the lentils. Even though Cinderella was not ready to attend the celebration, she received help from the birds who lived in the tree at her mother's grave. After receiving their help, Cinderella was ready to attend the celebration.

Neither the need to follow instructions nor Cinderella's unpreparedness for attending the celebration provides sufficient reason for prohibiting Cinderella from going to the celebration.

Cinderella should have gone to the celebration because she accepted the invitation, received permission, and suffered abandonment. By going to the celebration, Cinderella meets the prince who falls in love with her and wants to make her his wife.

## Type B: From *The Wind in the Willows*

"Something up above was calling him imperiously, and he made for the steep little tunnel." **Now that winter had ended, spring was moving through the air above and below the ground. Mole woke up one morning and began cleaning his home. As he cleaned, he felt something *carelessly calling* him to leave what he was doing and climb up out of his hole.**

Everyone agrees that a home provides comfort and protection, but some believe that Mole should have left his home and some believe that he should not have left his home. Mole should have left his safe, comfortable, and peaceful home for three reasons: He wanted to enjoy the new spring, to meet new friends, and to experience new adventures.

The first reason Mole should have left his safe, comfortable, and peaceful home is that he wanted to enjoy the new spring. While he was cleaning the house, Mole could sense something calling him. He hated a dirty home, but loved fresh air. Spring is like a newborn child. Mole wanted to climb up out of his home to enjoy the spring. Once out of his hole, he could experience the world above ground.

The second reason Mole should have left his safe, comfortable, and peaceful home is that he wanted to meet new friends. At home, Mole *lounged*, *lulled*, and *lived* alone. The first new friend Mole met, Ratty, lived on the river. Afterwards, Mole met Badger, who lived in the Wild Wood.

The third reason Mole should have left his safe, comfortable, and peaceful home is that he wanted to experience new adventures. Mole had never seen any home as nice as Toad Hall, where he ate lunch with Toad and Ratty. After lunch, Toad persuaded Mole to go on a road trip, where an automobile like a strong wind ran them off the road, into a ditch, and wrecked their cart. Mole also helped Toad save his home from the Weasels, who invaded Toad Hall while Toad served time in jail.

Some argue that Mole should not have left his home. The world above ground contained too many dangers. After leaving home, Mole fell out of Ratty's boat into the river. Later, he wandered into the Wild Wood, losing his way. Mole also risked losing his home to someone else who might have taken it. The possibility of danger does not make danger certain. Because something might happen does not mean that it will happen.

Others argue that Mole lacked patience. He threw down his brush before he finished cleaning his home. Mole lived safely and comfortably in his home free from any danger. The spring air distracted Mole from the security of his home. However, Mole's impatience is not a reason to stay home. It actually gives him more reason to leave his home for fresh air and a change.

Neither the possibility of danger nor Mole's impatience provide sufficient reason for Mole to have stayed home.

Mole should have left his safe, comfortable, and peaceful home because he wanted to enjoy the new spring, to meet new friends, and to experience new adventures. By leaving home, Mole learned how to make new friends whom he cared about and whom he could lift out of a snare when they fell into trouble.

## Type C: From *Julius Caesar*

What kind of man publicly celebrates his friend's life, but secretly plots his death? **Having completed his military campaigns with success, Caesar makes a bold move by returning to Rome and bringing his army with him. While Roman officials fear the possible outcome of Caesar's return, the people have crowded the streets to celebrate his recent arrival. Meanwhile, Cassius has been plotting with other senators to assassinate Caesar before he is crowned emperor. He needs to persuade one other senator, Brutus, to join their conspiracy. Cassius first unveils the senators' plan to Brutus in the streets during Caesar's grand entry. Though at first not favorable to the plan, Brutus is eventually won over by *Cassius' clever counsel.***

Every Roman agrees that Caesar is an important leader, but some believe that Brutus should not have stabbed Caesar and some believe that he should have stabbed Caesar. Brutus should not have stabbed Caesar for three reasons: Brutus served with fidelity, Caesar grew in popularity, and the conspirators acted in secret.

The first reason Brutus should not have stabbed Caesar is that Brutus served with fidelity. A good friend is as reliable as the sunrise. Caesar trusted Brutus with his life believing that with a friend such as Brutus there would never be an attempt to kill him. Not only did Caesar trust Brutus, but the Roman people also looked to Brutus as a respected and trustworthy leader of Rome.

The second reason Brutus should not have stabbed Caesar is that Caesar grew in popularity. Caesar returned to Rome as a hero in the eyes of the Roman people. The Romans loved and supported Caesar. In fact, they loved him so much that they desired to crown Caesar emperor. Yet, Caesar denied the crown three times for everyone to see.

The third reason Brutus should not have stabbed Caesar is that the conspirators acted in secret. Only some of the senators joined the plot to assassinate Caesar. Many of the senators knew nothing of the plot and played no part in carrying out this murderous act. Such secrecy avoided the possibility of conflict, of rejection, and of dismissal from opposing senators.

Some have argued that Brutus should have stabbed Caesar. Caesar was as sly as a fox. The ambitious leader led his army into the city, which not only threatened a free Rome, but marked the first steps toward tyranny. However, Caesar's lust for power required political action, not military. Brutus, not Caesar, turned the Senate floor into a battlefield.

Others argued that Brutus' love for Rome was greater than his love for Caesar. Caesar loved Rome no less than Brutus. The notion that Caesar threatened the liberty of Rome lacked sufficient evidence and emerged more from the irrational fears of a few men than the temperate love of the multitude.

Neither the argument that Caesar intended to use his military strength to enslave Rome nor the argument that Brutus acted out of a greater love than Caesar for the good of Rome provides sufficient reason for assassinating a man loved by those whom he served to protect.

Brutus should not have stabbed Caesar because Brutus served with fidelity, Caesar grew in popularity, and the conspirators acted in secret. The *riotous rage* of the *Roman* citizens sparked by Caesar's death will turn upon the murderous ban of guilty senators.

# ESSAY EIGHT: REVIEW PERSUASIVE ESSAY

I. Introduction
    A. Exordium
    B. Narratio
        1. Situation
        2. Actions
    C. Division
        1. Agreement
        2. Disagreement
            a. Thesis
            b. Counter-Thesis
    D. Distribution
        1. Thesis
        2. Enumeration
        3. Exposition
            a.
            b.
            c.

II. Proof
    A. Proof 1
        1.
        2.
        3.
    B. Proof 2
        1.
        2.
        3.
    C. Proof 3
        1.
        2.
        3.

III. Refutation
    A. Counter-Thesis
    B. Counter-Proof 1
        1. Summary of support for reason 1
        2. Inadequacy of reason 1
    C. Counter-Proof 2
        1. Summary of support for reason 2
        2. Inadequacy of reason 2
    D. Summary of Refutation

IV. Conclusion
    A. Thesis
    B. Summary of Proof
        1.
        2.
        3.
    C. Amplification
        1. To whom it matters
        2. Why it matters

# Type A: From *"Cinderella"*

Seize opportunity while it lasts. One spring the king wanted to find a wife for his son so he invited all of the beautiful girls in the kingdom to attend a three-day celebration. Cinderella asked her stepmother if she could go, but her stepmother told her that she was dirty, did not have a dress, and could not dance. After she begged to go, the stepmother dumped a bowl of lentils in a pile of ashes and said that she could go if all the lentils were cleaned in one hour. When Cinderella finished the task, her stepmother repeated that Cinderella could not go to the celebration.

Everyone agrees that Cinderella is invited to the celebration, but some believe that Cinderella should have gone to the celebration and some believe that she should not have gone to the celebration. Cinderella should have gone to the celebration for three reasons: She accepted the invitation, received permission, and suffered abandonment.

The first reason Cinderella should have gone to the celebration is that she accepted the invitation. Cinderella is as beautiful as a starry night. The king had invited all the beautiful girls in the kingdom to the palace for a three-day marriage celebration for his son. Cinderella hoped to dance at the celebration, but the prince desired to marry a young maid. She could possibly meet the prince, become his bride, and leave her home.

The second reason Cinderella should have gone to the celebration is that she received permission. After she asked, her stepmother promised to permit Cinderella to attend the celebration if she picked all the lentils out of the ashes within an hour. After Cinderella cleaned all the lentils with the help of the birds, her stepmother changed her mind as suddenly as a winding river. However, another bird helped Cinderella when it tossed down a dress out of the hazel tree for the celebration.

The third reason Cinderella should have gone to the celebration is that she suffered abandonment. Cinderella lived with her father, stepmother, and stepsisters. Her stepmother and stepsisters abused her, but she served them without complaint. They mocked the meek Cinderella and maliciously mistreated her. *Cinderella's father is a stag*, abandoning his offspring to the care of the herd.

Some argue that Cinderella should not have gone to the celebration. She needs to follow instructions. Her stepmother told her to stay home, and her real mother instructed her to be good. Cinderella must obey her parents. However, Cinderella was unfairly prohibited from attending the celebration by her stepmother, who despised her. Her *stepmother was a cat toying* with Cinderella by keeping her home for no just reason.

Others argue that Cinderella was not ready to go to the celebration. She did not have a dress and she did not know how to dance. Also, Cinderella did not clean the lentils herself. The birds helped her by cleaning all of the lentils. Even though Cinderella was not ready to attend the celebration, she received help from the birds who lived in the tree at her mother's grave. After receiving their help, Cinderella was ready to attend the celebration.

Neither the need to follow instructions nor Cinderella's unpreparedness for attending the celebration provides sufficient reason for prohibiting Cinderella from going to the celebration.

Cinderella should have gone to the celebration because she accepted the invitation, received permission, and suffered abandonment. By going to the celebration, Cinderella meets the prince who falls in love with her and wants to make her his wife.

## Type B: From *The Wind in the Willows*

"Something up above was calling him imperiously, and he made for the steep little tunnel." Now that winter had ended, spring was moving through the air above and below the ground. Mole woke up one morning and began cleaning his home. As he cleaned, he felt something carelessly calling him to leave what he was doing and climb up out of his hole.

Everyone agrees that a home provides comfort and protection, but some believe that Mole should have left his home and some believe that he should not have left his home. Mole should have left his safe, comfortable, and peaceful home for three reasons: He wanted to enjoy the new spring, to meet new friends, and to experience new adventures.

The first reason Mole should have left his safe, comfortable, and peaceful home is that he wanted to enjoy the new spring. While he was cleaning the house, Mole could sense something calling him. He hated a dirty home, but loved fresh air. Spring is like a newborn child. Mole wanted to climb up out of his home to enjoy the spring. Once out of his hole, he could experience the world above ground.

The second reason Mole should have left his safe, comfortable, and peaceful home is that he wanted to meet new friends. At home, Mole lounged, lulled, and lived alone. The first new friend Mole met, Ratty, lived on the river. Afterwards, Mole met Badger, who lived in the Wild Wood. *Good friends are a supportive bulwark* that protects against many dangers.

The third reason Mole should have left his safe, comfortable, and peaceful home is that he wanted to experience new adventures. Mole had never seen any home as nice as Toad Hall, where he ate lunch with Toad and Ratty. After lunch, Toad persuaded Mole to go on a road trip, where an automobile like a strong wind ran them off the road, into a ditch, and wrecked their cart. Mole also helped Toad save his home from the Weasels, who invaded Toad Hall while Toad served time in jail.

Some argue that Mole should not have left his home. The world above ground contained too many dangers. After leaving home, Mole fell out of Ratty's boat into the river. Later, he wandered into the Wild Wood, losing his way. Mole also risked losing his home to someone else who might have taken it. The possibility of danger does not make danger certain. Because something might happen does not mean that it will happen.

Others argue that Mole lacked patience. He threw down his brush before he finished cleaning his home. Mole lived safely and comfortably in his home free from any danger. The spring air distracted Mole from the security of his home. However, Mole's impatience is not a reason to stay home. *It is a favorable wind* driving Mole to leave his home for fresh air and a change.

Neither the possibility of danger nor Mole's impatience provides sufficient reason for Mole to have stayed home.

Mole should have left his safe, comfortable, and peaceful home because he wanted to enjoy the new spring, to meet new friends, and to experience new adventures. By leaving home, Mole learned how to make new friends whom he cared about and whom he could lift out of a snare when they fell into trouble.

## Type C: From *Julius Caesar*

What kind of man publicly celebrates his friend's life, but secretly plots his death? Having completed his military campaigns with success, Caesar makes a bold move by returning to Rome and bringing his army with him. While Roman officials fear the possible outcome of Caesar's return, the people have crowded the streets to celebrate his recent arrival. Meanwhile, Cassius has been plotting with other senators to assassinate Caesar before he is crowned emperor. He needs to persuade one other senator, Brutus, to join their conspiracy. Cassius first unveils the senators' plan to Brutus in the streets during Caesar's grand entry. Though at first not favorable to the plan, Brutus is eventually won over by Cassius' clever counsel.

Every Roman agrees that Caesar is an important leader, but some believe that Brutus should not have stabbed Caesar and some believe that he should have stabbed Caesar. Brutus should not have stabbed Caesar for three reasons: Brutus served with fidelity, Caesar grew in popularity, and the conspirators acted in secret.

The first reason Brutus should not have stabbed Caesar is that Brutus served with fidelity. A good friend is as reliable as the sunrise. Caesar trusted Brutus with his life believing that with a friend such as Brutus there would never be an attempt to kill him. Not only did Caesar trust Brutus, but the Roman people also looked to Brutus as a respected and trustworthy leader of Rome.

The second reason Brutus should not have stabbed Caesar is that Caesar grew in popularity. Caesar returned *to his flock* in Rome as a hero. The Romans loved and supported Caesar. In fact, they loved him so much that they desired to crown Caesar emperor. Yet, Caesar denied the crown three times for everyone to see.

The third reason Brutus should not have stabbed Caesar is that the conspirators acted in secret. Only some of the senators joined the plot to assassinate Caesar. Many of *the senators were startled squirrels* knowing nothing of the plot and played no part in carrying out this murderous act. Such secrecy avoided the possibility of conflict, of rejection, and of dismissal from opposing senators.

Some have argued that Brutus should have stabbed Caesar. Caesar was as sly as a fox. The ambitious leader led his army into the city, which not only threatened a free Rome, but marked the first steps toward tyranny. However, Caesar's lust for power required political action, not military. Brutus, not Caesar, turned the Senate floor into a battlefield.

Others argued that Brutus' love for Rome was greater than his love for Caesar. Caesar loved Rome no less than Brutus. The notion that Caesar threatened the liberty of Rome lacked sufficient evidence and emerged more from the irrational fears of a few men than the temperate love of the multitude.

Neither the argument that Caesar intended to use his military strength to enslave Rome nor the argument that Brutus acted out of a greater love than Caesar for the good of Rome provides sufficient reason for assassinating a man loved by those whom he served to protect.

Brutus should not have stabbed Caesar because Brutus served with fidelity, Caesar grew in popularity, and the conspirators acted in secret. The riotous rage of the Roman citizens sparked by Caesar's death will turn upon the murderous ban of guilty senators.

# ESSAY NINE: REVIEW PERSUASIVE ESSAY

I. Introduction
    A. Exordium
    B. Narratio
        1. Situation
        2. Actions
    C. Division
        1. Agreement
        2. Disagreement
            a. Thesis
            b. Counter-Thesis
    D. Distribution
        1. Thesis
        2. Enumeration
        3. Exposition
            a.
            b.
            c.

II. Proof
    A. Proof 1
        1.
        2.
        3.
    B. Proof 2
        1.
        2.
        3.
    C. Proof 3
        1.
        2.
        3.

III. Refutation
    A. Counter-Thesis
    B. Counter-Proof 1
        1. Summary of support for reason 1
        2. Inadequacy of reason 1
    C. Counter-Proof 2
        1. Summary of support for reason 2
        2. Inadequacy of reason 2
    D. Summary of Refutation

IV. Conclusion
    A. Thesis
    B. Summary of Proof
        1.
        2.
        3.
    C. Amplification
        1. To whom it matters
        2. Why it matters

# Type A: From *"Cinderella"*

Seize opportunity while it lasts. One spring the king wanted to find a wife for his son so he invited all of the beautiful girls in the kingdom to attend a three-day celebration. Cinderella asked her stepmother if she could go, but her stepmother told her that she was dirty, did not have a dress, and could not dance. After she begged to go, the stepmother dumped a bowl of lentils in a pile of ashes and said that she could go if all the lentils were cleaned in one hour. When Cinderella finished the task, her stepmother repeated that Cinderella could not go to the celebration.

Everyone agrees that Cinderella is invited to the celebration, but some believe that Cinderella should have gone to the celebration and some believe that she should not have gone to the celebration. Cinderella should have gone to the celebration for three reasons: She accepted the invitation, received permission, and suffered abandonment.

The first reason Cinderella should have gone to the celebration is that she accepted the invitation. Cinderella is as beautiful as a starry night. The king had invited all the beautiful girls in the kingdom to the palace for a three-day marriage celebration for his son. Cinderella hoped to dance at the celebration, but the prince desired to marry a young maid. She could *meet* the prince, *seek* her freedom, and *leave* her home.

The second reason Cinderella should have gone to the celebration is that she received permission. After she asked, her stepmother promised to permit Cinderella to attend the celebration if she picked all the lentils out of the ashes within an hour. After Cinderella cleaned all the lentils with the help of the birds, her stepmother changed her mind as suddenly as a winding river. However, another bird helped Cinderella when it tossed down a dress out of the hazel tree for the celebration.

The third reason Cinderella should have gone to the celebration is that she suffered abandonment. Cinderella lived with her father, stepmother, and stepsisters. Her new family *tortured* her, but she *served* them without *further* complaint. They mocked the meek Cinderella and maliciously mistreated her. Cinderella's father is a stag, abandoning his offspring to the care of the herd.

Some argue that Cinderella should not have gone to the celebration. She needs to follow instructions. Her stepmother told her to stay home, and her real mother instructed her to be good. Cinderella must obey her parents. However, Cinderella was unfairly prohibited from attending the celebration by her stepmother, who despised her. Her stepmother was a cat toying with Cinderella by keeping her home for no just reason.

Others argue that Cinderella was not ready to go to the celebration. She did not have a dress and she did not know how to dance. Also, Cinderella did not clean the lentils herself. The birds helped her by cleaning all of the lentils. Even though Cinderella was not ready to attend the celebration, she received help from the birds who lived in the tree at her mother's grave. After receiving their help, Cinderella was ready to attend the celebration.

Neither the need to follow instructions nor Cinderella's unpreparedness for attending the celebration provides sufficient reason for prohibiting Cinderella from going to the celebration.

Cinderella should have gone to the celebration because she accepted the invitation, received permission, and suffered abandonment. By going to the celebration, Cinderella meets the prince who falls in love with her and wants to make her his wife.

Neither the need to follow instructions nor Cinderella's unpreparedness for attending the celebration provides sufficient reason for prohibiting Cinderella from going to the celebration.

Cinderella should have gone to the celebration because she accepted the invitation, received permission, and suffered abandonment. By going to the celebration, Cinderella meets the prince who falls in love with her and wants to make her his wife.

## Type B: From *The Wind in the Willows*

Something up above was calling him imperiously, and he made for the steep little tunnel." Now that winter had ended, spring was moving through the air above and below the ground. Mole woke up one morning and began cleaning his home. As he cleaned, he felt something carelessly calling him to leave what he was doing and climb up out of his hole.

Everyone agrees that a home provides comfort and protection, but some believe that Mole should have left his home and some believe that he should not have left his home. Mole should have left his safe, comfortable, and peaceful home for three reasons: He wanted to enjoy the new spring, to meet new friends, and to experience new adventures.

The first reason Mole should have left his safe, comfortable, and peaceful home is that he wanted to enjoy the new spring. While he was cleaning the house, Mole could sense something calling him. He hated a dirty home, but loved fresh air. Spring is like a newborn child. Mole wanted to climb up out of his home to enjoy the spring. Once out of his hole, he could experience the world above ground.

The second reason Mole should have left his safe, comfortable, and peaceful home is that he wanted to meet new friends. At home, Mole lounged, lulled, and lived alone. The first new friend Mole *visited*, Ratty, *lived* on and *in* and near the *river*. Afterwards, Mole met Badger, who lived in the Wild Wood. Good friends are a supportive bulwark that protects against many dangers.

The third reason Mole should have left his safe, comfortable, and peaceful home is that he wanted to experience new adventures. Mole had never seen any home as nice as Toad Hall, where he ate lunch with Toad and Ratty. After lunch, Toad persuaded Mole to go on a road trip, where an automobile like a strong wind ran them off the road, into a ditch, and wrecked their cart. Mole also helped Toad save his home from the Weasels who invaded Toad Hall while Toad served time in jail.

Some argue that Mole should not have left his home. The world above ground contained too many dangers. After leaving home, Mole fell out of Ratty's boat into the river. Later, he wandered into the Wild Wood losing his way. Mole also risked losing his home to someone else who might have taken it. The possibility of danger does not make danger certain. Because something might happen does not mean that it will happen.

Others argue that Mole lacked patience. He threw down his brush before he finished cleaning his home. Mole lived safely and comfortably in his home free from any danger. The spring air distracted Mole from the security of his home. However, Mole's impatience is not a reason to stay home. It is a favorable wind driving Mole to leave his home for fresh air and a change.

Neither the possibility of danger nor Mole's impatience provides sufficient reason for Mole to have stayed home.

Mole should have left his safe, comfortable, and peaceful home because he wanted to enjoy the new spring, to meet new friends, and to experience new adventures. By leaving home, Mole learned how to make new friends whom he cared about and whom he could lift *up* out of a *rough* spot when they *stumbled* into *trouble*.

## Type C: From *Julius Caesar*

What kind of man publicly celebrates his friend's life, but secretly plots his death? Having completed his military campaigns with success, Caesar makes a bold move by returning to Rome and bringing his army with him. While Roman officials fear the possible outcome of Caesar's return, the people have crowded the streets to celebrate his recent arrival. Meanwhile, Cassius has been plotting with other senators to assassinate Caesar before he is crowned emperor. He needs to persuade one other senator, Brutus, to join their conspiracy. Cassius first unveils the senators' plan to Brutus in the streets during Caesar's grand entry. Though at first not favorable to the plan, Brutus is eventually won over by Cassius' clever counsel.

Every Roman agrees that *Caesar* is an important and *fearless leader*, but some believe that Brutus should not have stabbed Caesar and some believe that he should have stabbed Caesar. Brutus should not have stabbed Caesar for three reasons: Brutus served with fidelity, Caesar grew in popularity, and the conspirators acted in secret.

The first reason Brutus should not have stabbed Caesar is that Brutus served with fidelity. A good friend is as reliable as the sunrise. Caesar trusted Brutus with his life believing that with a friend such as Brutus there would never be an attempt to kill him. Not only did Caesar trust Brutus, but the Roman people also looked to Brutus as a respected and trustworthy leader of Rome.

The second reason Brutus should not have stabbed Caesar is that Caesar grew in popularity. Caesar returned to his flock in Rome as a hero. The Romans loved and supported Caesar. In fact, they loved him so much that they desired to crown Caesar emperor. Yet, Caesar denied the crown three times for everyone to see.

The third reason Brutus should not have stabbed Caesar is that the conspirators acted in secret. Only some of the senators joined the plot to assassinate Caesar. Many of the senators were startled squirrels knowing nothing of the plot and played no part in carrying out this murderous act. Such secrecy avoided the possibility of conflict, of rejection, and of dismissal from opposing senators.

Some have argued that Brutus should have stabbed Caesar. Caesar was as sly as a fox. The ambitious *head led* his *steady* army into the city, which not only *threatened* a free Rome, but *sped* towards the first *steps* of tyranny. However, Caesar's lust for power required political action, not military. Brutus, not Caesar, turned the Senate floor into a battlefield.

Others argued that Brutus' love for Rome was greater than his love for Caesar. Caesar loved Rome no less than Brutus. The notion that Caesar threatened the liberty of Rome lacked sufficient evidence and emerged more from the irrational fears of a few men than the temperate love of the multitude.

Neither the argument that Caesar intended to use his military strength to enslave Rome nor the argument that Brutus acted out of a greater love than Caesar for the good of Rome provides sufficient reason for assassinating a man loved by those whom he served to protect.

Brutus should not have stabbed Caesar because Brutus served with fidelity, Caesar grew in popularity, and the conspirators acted in secret. The riotous rage of the Roman citizens sparked by Caesar's death will turn upon the murderous ban of guilty senators.

Part Five
# Glossary

**Adverb.** A word used to modify the meaning of a verb, adjective, participle, or an adverb.

**Agent.** The thing which does the action expressed in the verb.

**Alliteration.** The repetition of the same letter at the beginning of two or more adjacent words.

**Amplification.** Part of an essay's conclusion in which the writer states to whom his issue matters, and why it matters to that person or group.

**Antecedent.** An event that precedes another event, but does not necessarily cause it. We think about the antecedent when we apply the topic of relation to the issue. "Ante" is from Latin, meaning "before." "Cede" is from Latin, meaning "to go."

**Antithesis.** The opposition of words and sentiments contained in the same sentence, often in parallel structure.

**ANI.** A three-column chart used to collect reasons that AFFIRM (A) or NEGATE (N) the issue. The third column, I, functions much like an inbox and allows you to store any INTERESTING or INDETERMINATE bit of information.

**Assonance.** The repetition of similar vowel sounds, preceded and followed by different consonants, in the stressed syllables of adjacent words.

**Authority.** One of the five common topics. It asks the question, "Who says what about this subject?" (e.g., What does the Bible say? What do my parents say?) A research paper is written mainly with the topic of authority.

**Circumstance.** One of the five common topics. It asks the question, "What is happening at the time or place of the issue or term?"

**Clause.** A syntactical construction containing a subject and a predicate.

**Comparison.** One of the five common topics. We ask questions about how things are similar, and then about how they are different.

**Comparison by Degree.** Degree measures quantity in terms of more and less.

**Comparison by Kind.** Kind compares the quality of one thing to another in terms of better or worse.

**Conclusion.** Wraps up the essay by reviewing the argument the essay has presented.

**Consequent.** An action that follows an event. This is part of the topic of relation.

**Counter-thesis.** A statement that opposes the thesis.

**Definition.** One of the five common topics. A definition of a word sets the limits within which a word has meaning. A definition of a thing identifies the genus and differentia of the thing defined. Definition asks the questions, "To what category does a thing belong?" "How does it compare to other members of that set?" "What are its parts or aspects?" A formal definition states the genus (group) and differentia (unique qualities) of a term.

**Differentia.** In the topic of Definition, we ask what category our subject belongs to, and then how it is different from other members of the group it is in; the differences between a term and the other members of its genus are its differentia.

**Division.** A precise statement of the agreement and disagreement between the writer and an opponent.

**Effect.** The result of an action or cause.

**Enumeration.** The number of reasons the essay presents in support of its thesis.

**Exordium.** The opening of an essay or speech, the first part of the introduction. Its purpose is to connect the reader to the material of the essay.

**Exposition.** A statement that presents the main points that make up the essay's proof.

**Genus.** The category or group to which the thing defined belongs; the first part of a term's definition.

**Introduction.** The opening to an essay.

**Issue.** A statement that asks whether someone should do something.

**Main Proof.** The main reasons that support the thesis. Each main proof is in turn supported by three "sub-proofs" or supporting proofs. You draw the main proofs from the sorted A or N column. After you sorted the ANI, you provided a heading for each group that you categorized. Once you select the three groups you will use in defense of your thesis, the headings you assigned to each group are the main proofs.

**Metaphor.** A trope in which an object, action, character, or thing is compared indirectly with another object, action, or thing of a different kind (e.g., "All the world's a stage...").

**Narratio.** Narrative; also called a "statement of facts" or "statement of circumstances." It tells a story, with settings, actors, and actions, to inform the reader about the circumstances they need to know about the subject, or thesis, of the essay.

**Parallelism.** A scheme in which two or more words, phrases, or clauses are aligned in such a way that the parts of speech in each line up with the same parts of speech in the other words, phrases, or clauses. Parallelism gives harmonious form, interest, and beauty to a sentence or passage. Parts of a term. The qualities, attributes, and characteristics (oftentimes physical) associated with the term. What are the parts of the term "Edmund"? He has a mind, a body, a spirit, wills, and the ability to reason. He is male, is a brother, is jealous, is curious, is a son, and so on.

**Passive voice.** A verb form or voice in which the grammatical subject receives the verb's action.

**Patient.** The thing which receives the action expressed in the verb.

**Phonogram.** A single letter or a fixed combination of two, three, or four letters, which is the symbol for one sound in a given word.

**Phrase.** Two or more words joined together to form a grammatical unit.

**Preposition.** A word used to show the relationship between its object and some other word.

**Proofs.** The reasons you will present to defend this thesis.

**Refutation.** The response to an opposing argument. For a persuasive essay, you will anticipate two arguments that your opponent will have against your thesis. A refutation states those two reasons and explains why they are inadequate.

**Relation.** One of the five common topics, relation includes questions about cause and effect, and antecedent and consequent.

**Simile.** A trope that forms an explicit comparison of two things that are of a different kind but share a striking quality. Similes use "like," "as," or "seem" to make a comparison explicit.

**Subject.** "The subject of a proposition is that of which something is affirmed." —Thomas W. Harvey

**Sub-proof.** LTW may also call the sub-proof a "supporting proof." The supports are the specific evidence, argument, or authority that supports the three main proofs. You determine the three sub-proofs for each main proof from the three groups you selected in the sorted A or N column. Each group should have several reasons listed from which you choose three to use as the supporting proofs.

**Terms.** Words or expressions used to name things.

**Thesis.** The statement of the proposition the essay will defend. If the essay's issue is "Whether Edmund should have followed the White Witch" and you are taking the negative side of the issue, then your thesis is "Edmund should not have followed the White Witch."

**Topics.** Questions we ask in order to come up with something to say when we write. Based on the Greek word for "topic," the "common topics" are places you go to discover information. These places refer to the kinds of questions asked during the invention stage of writing.

**Vague verb.** A non-specific verb that leaves out important information.